AUSTRALIA'S MOST
MURDEROUS
PRISON

JAMES PHELPS

AUSTRALIA'S MOST MURDEROUS PRISON

BEHIND THE WALLS OF GOULBURN JAIL

EBURY
PRESS

An Ebury Press book
Published by Random House Australia Pty Ltd
Level 3, 100 Pacific Highway, North Sydney NSW 2060
www.randomhouse.com.au

Penguin
Random House
Australia

First published by Ebury Press in 2015

National Library of Australia
Cataloguing-in-Publication Entry

Phelps, James, author.
Australia's most murderous prison/James Phelps.

ISBN 978 0 85798 749 5 (paperback)

Goulburn Correctional Centre.
Prisons – New South Wales – Goulburn.
Correctional personnel – New South Wales – Goulburn.
Correctional personnel – Violence against – New South Wales – Goulburn.
Prisons – New South Wales – Goulburn – Security measures.
Prisoners – New South Wales – Goulburn.
Prison violence – New South Wales – Goulburn.

365.99447

Cover design by Luke Causby/Blue Cork
Cover photo © News Ltd/Newspix
Internal design and typesetting by Midland Typesetters, Australia
Printed in Australia by Griffin Press, an accredited ISO AS/NZS 14001:2004 Environmental
Management System printer

Random House Australia uses papers that are natural, renewable and recyclable products and
made from wood grown in sustainable forests. The logging and manufacturing processes are
expected to conform to the environmental regulations of the country of origin.

This book is for Iris Phelps – the greatest woman I have ever known

Contents

1

WELCOME TO GOULBURN

A Shitty Reception

The famous fish was finally here.

'Hey Dad!' the inmate yelled. 'Cop this, you kiddy-fiddling fuck.'

Smack! Shit slapped against Robert Hughes's face, the faecal blow forcing his cowardly eyes from the concrete and into the crowd.

'Keep walking, Hughes,' screamed a Goulburn guard, the safety of the wing sheltering him from the flying shit. 'Move!'

Hughes took another step.

Smash! A urine-filled milk carton crashed into his shoulder, stinking yellow liquid splattered his face.

'Hey Dad!' screamed another. 'Why don't you *pissssssss* off?'

Judge Peter Zahra predicted the 'brazen' and 'predatory' Hughes would be at 'significant risk of harm from other prisoners when he sentenced the star of the famous Australian sitcom *Hey Dad...!* to a maximum of ten years' jail for indecently assaulting four victims, including a child co-star.

And he was right . . .

The smirk – the one Hughes wore throughout his trial, even when he was sentenced – was now gone. A carton containing shit had slapped it from his face.

'This is Goulburn, mate,' said one of the 30 or so inmates crossing the concrete yard called 'the Circle', a section in the middle of the prison compound that connects all the jails together. 'What did you expect?'

The inmate pushed Hughes in the back. 'You walk ahead,' he continued. 'We're going to hang back a bit.'

Hughes looked to the end of the yard.

It's only 40 metres. Not that far.

He then looked to his right where another 30 general population inmates eyeballed him from behind a wire yard fence.

Are they holding milk cartons?

He looked to his left – more inmates stood behind another fence, all tattoos, muscles and jail-yard tough.

Yep. They're milk cartons, and they're filled with shit.

Robert Hughes pissed his pants. And then he was given Goulburn jail's shittiest-ever reception.

'They just unloaded,' recalled a Goulburn guard. 'Piss and poo – they covered him in it. It was his first day in Goulburn and he was brought out into the yard. I was standing on the Circle. Hughes was a protection inmate because of his crimes. He was never going to be put in, or out, with general population inmates because they would have killed him. But while he wasn't going into a yard with them, he had to walk through the fenced-off corridor between two other yards to get to an area called the Cookhouse before being let into the activities yard.'

The 40-metre chain-gang march from one prison block to the next was usually uneventful. But an exception was made for Hughes that afternoon; his fame and his crime made him an irresistible substitute sewer.

'I'm not sure how they knew he was coming,' the officer continued. 'But they knew. And they had all armed them-selves up with shit and gone out to meet him. He was in the yellow yard, which is strict, strict protection. He was with all the rock spiders and paedophiles and was safe from them, but he wasn't safe from anything that could be thrown over or through the fence.'

The Goulburn guards did not have time to protect Hughes from the shit-storm. Or maybe they just didn't want to.

'When Robert Hughes came out of that wing I would estimate 50 to 70 inmates all ran to the yard,' the officer said. 'We thought, *Oh shit, it is on here.* Before we knew it he had shit and piss thrown on him from the time he walked into the yard to the time he walked out of the back of the yard. What they do is shit and then piss in the little milk contain-ers they're issued, and then they put their arms through the bars and fling it. You would be really surprised how far.

'Hughes was attacked from both sides – one was a protec-tion yard and the other a general yard. They were all into him. The other inmates did their best to let him go first.'

Covered from head to toe in human waste, Hughes sat on top of a small grassy hill in the activities yard.

And he cried.

'He would have tried to clean himself up,' the officer said, 'but it was impossible without having a shower. He spent the entire time sitting on the hill, sooking. He was a stinking mess.'

Then he was sent back to his cell; first to the Cookhouse and then back through the yard.

'It happened again on the way back,' the officer said. 'They had reloaded and come back for more.'

Hughes held the phone against his ear.

'I can't do it,' he sobbed to his partner on the other end of the line. 'This place is horrible. I thought I would be okay, but I can't stay here. I can't stay in Goulburn. This place is hell. You have to get me out.'

A Goulburn officer overheard his conversation.

'He was crying like a baby,' the officer said. 'He was on the phone to his missus, the one that stood by him, and he was like, "I was covered in shit and piss today." It was one of the funniest phone calls ever. He had just been issued his prison greens. He was a big girl through the reception process, sobbing the whole time, begging to go back to Silverwater [Correctional Centre].'

But Hughes was not transferred, his tearful pleas falling on deaf ears. And unfortunately for Hughes – not his victims – the prison punishment from his peers continued.

'He is the only inmate in Goulburn who wears a jacket in summer,' another Goulburn officer said. 'He walks around when it's 40 degrees wearing a ski jacket.'

Why?

'To stop his shirts being stained by piss,' the officer continued. 'Not just that, but spit. The inmates are more opportunistic now; they will throw whatever they have when they see him. If they have nothing, which is most often the case, then they will just spit.'

They also yell; an inmate recently split bellies with eight witty words.

'He was walking back from muster across the Circle in early February [2014], getting sent back into his wing,' revealed an officer. 'He was wearing this big fucking jacket on a 40-degree day. All was quiet and nothing was going on. It was one of the funniest things I can remember in the last year ... You have to picture it. This big Aboriginal bloke broke the silence by getting up against the fence and scream-ing, "I'm a celebrity ... Get me out of here." The whole yard fell over laughing because they had all been watching the reality show by the same name that had just started on TV.

'Robert just went red, kept on walking like it wasn't meant for him.'

Hughes isn't the only inmate who has broken down in the Goulburn Correctional Centre, a high-security 'hell hole' located in the picturesque Southern Highlands of New South Wales, about two hours away from Sydney. It is home to the worst criminals in Australia – serial killers, rapists, mass murderers, drug kingpins, gang bosses and terrorists, both convicted and aspiring.

Yep, the Goulburn Jail, opened 1 July 1884, is Australia's answer to Guantanamo Bay detention camp, with the 'Supermax' prison at the heart of the iron and sandstone institution. That's where the beasts live: Ivan Milat, Bassam Hamzy, Bilal Skaf and Khaled Cheikho.

You will meet them all soon . . .

Guarding Goulburn

Former Goulburn guard Mick Pezzano described the difficult conditions Goulburn prison presents, and the kind of grit you need to make it every day as a guard.

'I was the Manager of Classification at Goulburn prison for a number of years, and I was well-aware of the types of inmates that were classified to go there. Goulburn was regarded as the arsehole end of the world as far as an inmate was concerned. It wasn't because of its distance away from the Sydney metro region, but because of its reputation for being a hard, barren, ruthless prison.

'Basically, an inmate was sent to Goulburn because he was either a maximum-security rating or he was unable to be managed in another prison. It also serves as a reception prison to the local southern region. I recall many times the arguments we would have with staff at Goulburn when they were receiving inmates from other centres because they had been "tipped", which meant they had played up, were involved in a serious assault, were trafficking drugs, were a risk of escape, etc. More than likely they were placed on segregation, were regressed in classification and sent to Goulburn as some sort of punishment. Goulburn was regarded around the state as the prison that took any inmate who could not be managed at other centres. I never regarded an inmate being sent to Goulburn as a punishment; it was just that there were very little options where we could house maximum-security inmates at that period of time or separate them as such.

'On many occasions when I was classifying inmates to Goulburn they would literally go into shock; some of them would get aggressive and threaten the officers if they tried to send them there. Some would just crumble in fear at the thought, because of what they had been told by other inmates or what they already knew of the place. It had a reputation.

'Not only was it the end of the road with no turning back, but to then get out of Goulburn really took a lot of work and effort for an inmate – who was placed at Goulburn for his non-compliance and threat to the good order and safety of the prison – to be able to finally reduce in classification and eventually transfer out of there. For some inmates this took years, but eventually they got through. It was pleasing for us to see that inmates were able to progress while in custody, conform to the system and prepare themselves for eventual release back into the community. Unfortunately for some inmates at Goulburn, they never transferred out and remained there until their sentence had expired, a lot of them serving well into their parole period.

'Along with senior management, I would carefully scrutinise every recommendation and transfer application that came before us for an inmate to progress. Officers on the ground at Goulburn, who had the arduous task of supervising them day in and day out, also played a vital part in the management of the inmates.

'As bad as Goulburn was regarded by inmates, the officers who worked there knew their stuff – they are a well-organised and drilled unit. They have to be, the types of inmates there have nothing to lose, and it's not like working on a prison farm. I really respect the officers and admire their courage; they put their lives on the line daily.

'The Goulburn centre itself is an old jungle of concrete and steel yards and razor wire separating the various cultural groups. The wings and cells are old-style, with no showers in them like the modern-day prison cell. A lot of the assaults and stabbings happen in the shower block. As much as staff supervise and the installation of CCTV monitors are in place to assist them, it does not take long for an inmate to be bashed senseless and stabbed.

'The MPU (Multi-Purpose Unit) at Goulburn is also a well-run area. Basically staff have to manage inmates in that environment who cannot be managed anywhere else in the state. The 2002 Goulburn riot was a classic example of how dangerous prison can be – not only for inmates but for the officers who work there.

'This place is certainly the most violent jail in Australia, and it holds the most violent men.'

Lions and Legends

Never, ever look at the lion.

'Don't even take a peek,' said former Goulburn Jail Governor Allan Chisholm of the lion carved into the sandstone entrance arch. It hovers over the green iron gate, watching everyone who enters and leaves.

'There is an old superstition that if you look at it you are going to come back . . . as an inmate. No one looks at it. No one is game . . . just in case. The lion scares the shit out of the people.'

And so does this jail – an Australian legend full of fear and fright.

'I knew it was the roughest jail of them all, even before I got there,' said former Goulburn officer Ian Norris. 'My dad worked at Long Bay prison, and he was always telling me horror stories about Goulburn Jail. This is a place full of stories . . . I had served in the military, I went to Vietnam, and I thought I had seen everything. But I hadn't. I can remember the first day I walked into that place and thinking, *What the hell have I gotten myself into.* I can tell you from experience that all the stories are true.'

Goulburn Jail has had many names over the years. It has officially been called the Goulburn Reformatory, the Goulburn Training Centre and the Goulburn Correctional Centre (its current name).

Unofficially, it has been known as the Killing Fields, the HARM(U) and, as Pezzano put it, a 'hell hole' for inmates in the 'arse-end' of the prison world.

In fact, this place is so bad it scares serial offenders straight.

'The only good thing about Goulburn was that it made the worst inmates in other jails across the state become model prisoners because they were so afraid of being sent there,' said former high-ranking prison official Dave 'Emu' Farrell.

'Inmates were being murdered, guards were being bashed and stabbed, and there was just a terrible, terrible feeling in that jail. I remember walking through the yard and all I could hear was the sound of metal hitting concrete. It was the inmates dropping shivs [makeshift jail weapons]. We had metal detectors but still couldn't find them all. They were all armed up and ready to kill.

'You really had to have done something bad to end up there. Rapists and killers like the Murphy brothers are here, and gang rapists like Bilal Skaf are here.'

There are also ex-commando contract killers, arsonists, paedophiles and five men who tried to blow up a nuclear reactor in Sydney.

Soon you will meet them too . . .

The Ghost and the Gallows

Norris was beat; eight hours on his feet had his back screaming sore.

A quick rest will do the trick. Ten minutes off my feet and I will be fine.

And why not? The night senior had just checked the wing and the inmates were all safely locked up. They were dreaming in the dark.

'So I pulled out the chair and sat down at the desk that was in the old B Wing office,' Norris recalled. 'I decided to listen to the night. To hear if there was anything going on.'

Norris leaned back in the chair. *Peace at last.*

'And then I heard singing,' Norris said. 'Gentle, soft singing and the strum of a guitar.'

Norris sat up – so did the hairs on the back of his neck.

'We had just done a ramp [a raid where contraband is seized] early that day, so nobody had guitars or radios. There was nothing in that wing and everybody was asleep.'

Norris pushed away the chair and looked down at the out-of-place rug beneath him. He realised where he was standing, well, more like *what* he was standing on . . .

'The old trapdoor,' Norris said. 'Right under the gallows. It was the assistant superintendent's office, and they had just thrown a rug over it and sat the desk on top.'

He stood and listened with an equal measure of curiosity and fear.

'It sounded like a really old song,' Norris said. 'Like an early Aussie folk song. It was nothing I had ever heard before, but it was really harrowing.'

He listened harder; still curious, still scared.

'I got up and walked towards the noise,' Norris said, 'out onto the landing and then to a door. I opened it and walked into a corridor, and I was standing in front of one of the two condemned cells.'

The noise was coming from a cell that hadn't been used for over 100 years – since 5 December 1900, to be precise.

Norris pushed open the old cell door and the music stopped. All of a sudden, gone.

'There was nothing in there. Just a tiny little cell. Absolutely empty.'

Norris turned . . . and ran.

'I got out of there quick-smart,' Norris said. 'I was freaked. I didn't believe in ghosts until then.'

I asked Norris about the ghost, who it could have been.

'There was only one bloke ever hung in Goulburn, from what I can gather,' Norris said. 'And I don't know who or when – I don't know anything – but I do know on that night, and I will swear on a stack of Bibles, I heard somebody in that cell, the first condemned cell, gently singing and playing his guitar. It scared the willies out of me.'

The only man to be executed in Goulburn Jail was, in fact, John Sleigh. He spent his final night alive in a tiny first-floor cell located at the south-eastern end of B Wing. It was, of course, the condemned cell described by Norris.

Sleigh was sentenced to death for shooting Frank Curran dead at Back Creek before burning his body. And he was hanged at 9 am on 5 December 1900.

'The drop was some twenty feet from the door of my cell,' described James Dwyer, a Goulburn inmate on the day of Sleigh's execution. 'It has always been a spot that held my attention each time I climbed to my whitewashed home. All through the night before he died, the condemned sang songs that were heard by all the prisoners in the wing. [Sleigh] had a fine baritone voice and his words rang through the big building. They were songs of the day. He chanted "Annie Rooney", "Dreaming of Home", "Mary Green" and other favourites. The Governor ordered him to stop, telling him he was upsetting the nerves of other prisoners around him, but the songster took no notice of the command. I really didn't see any reason why he should. Outside the cell of the condemned, and quite within hearing of the wretch inside, the hangman and his assistants were testing the rope by tying a bag of sand the exact weight of the man to be hanged and letting it drop with awful clatter. No prisoner slept that night.'

And it appears, if Norris is to be believed, that Sleigh continues to ignore the governor, singing now to deprive guards of sleep rather than inmates.

Norris is stunned when I tell him who the executed inmate was – more so when I say what he was doing on the night before he died.

'Bugger me. That's exactly what I heard. I heard him singing. That's really spooky. I never thought to look it up.'

Goulburn, however, was a place of death long before the singing Sleigh swung.

Ever heard of a gibbet?

Bleached Bones

General Sir Richard Bourke (yep, the guy *every* Bourke Street in Australia is named after and the first man in the colony to be honoured with a public statue) jumped as his wife, horrified and hastily lashing out, pinched his arm.

The Governor of New South Wales winced – *the governess had got him good.*

'Abhorrent,' he shouted, not at her but at the men proudly showing him the sun-bleached bones. 'Remove them at once.'

He turned his back on the gruesome gibbet after promising the governess it would be gone.

'Barbaric,' he said. 'This will never happen again.'

Bourke then declared gibbeting illegal and ordered the structure to be sawn down and destroyed. Sure, public hangings were still okay, but you could no longer display a body in a metal cage and leave it to rot above a city street.

The legend of Goulburn justice began that year, 1833, as the decomposing corpses of John White and William Mooney – sentenced to death by hanging 12 months earlier for murdering overseer Maurice Roach with an axe – were left as food for the hungry hawks and crows that circled above.

The township of Goulburn was first established in 1820, four residential blocks erected around a square on a bend of the Wollondilly River. The first substantial building was the lock-up: a ramshackle structure of wood, eight metres long by three metres wide. The jail soon fell down and was rebuilt with more wood, but this time on a concrete slab. It was officially called Goulburn Plains Gaol and referred to as the 'wicker basket'. The jail was still nothing more than a hut with a door – no windows and the wooden logs so loosely lashed together that prisoners often slipped through the gaps and escaped into the nearby paddock.

And, of course, there were the instruments of death and dissuasion in plain sight on a clear rise at the back of the township.

'Prisoners sentenced to death were hanged or "turned off" on the gallows and then, when considered appropriate, hung from the gibbet in an iron cage,' described Dr James Kerr in a 1994 Goulburn Jail conservation plan commissioned by the NSW Department of Public Planning for the Department of Corrective Services. 'The intention being to hold the carcass together and exhibit it as a measure of discouragement to other evildoers.'

'The execution of these two miserable wretches shocked,' reported the *Goulburn Herald* at the time. 'Their bodies were gibbetted on the rising ground on the north-west side of Goulburn, a spot which has ever since been known as Gallows Hill.'

Governor Bourke might have stopped the gibbeting 12 months later, but the killing continued . . .

A man called Whitton was next; he was hanged outside the Auburn Street lock-up for the crime of bushranging. And then came James Talbot in 1854, who had the dubious honour of being the first man hanged in the all-new 1841 masonry-built prison.

The 1841 census showed the old Auburn Street lock-up was bursting at the seams with 50 male inmates sharing the hut with a lone law-breaking woman. So a new jail was built and they were moved. This prison, officially finished in

1845 – four years after occupation began – had over 40 cells stacked over two floors. There was also a three-room narthex with entry lobby, warders' office, gatehouse, cookhouse and cesspool.

Still, the jail was small and crime was large.

The 'new' prison was decommissioned just 39 years after it was opened, razed to the ground in 1884. Enter the Goulburn Jail that stands today – all legendary lions, ghosts and gallows.

The Gaol at Goulburn, as it was officially known, was opened on 1 July 1884. Designed by Colonial Architect James Barnett, the $61,000 super prison had four radial cell wings, eight yards, a chapel and a detached hospital.

'Constructed of local brick with stone dressing, it was finished with handsome architectural detailing,' Kerr's conservation plan reported. 'Goulburn, for the first time in Australia, had single cells of reasonable size (3.96 metres by 2.13 metres). These were based on the cell dimensions of England's famous Pentonville [Prison] model.'

This is the prison where Sleigh was hanged. And it is the prison he still haunts today. The 1884 jail is the historic epicentre of today's Goulburn Correctional Centre that has grown to include the X Wing (1968), the High-Security Dispersal Unit (1980), the Multi-Purpose Unit (1986) and the Supermax (2001).

The prison housed first-time offenders from 1928 to 1949; now it is home to Australia's most evil and violent men.

But first, let's talk a walk through the 'Killing Fields'.

Welcome to Goulburn Jail – Australia's most murderous prison . . .

2

THE KILLING FIELDS

Slice, Slash and Scurry: The Slaughter Starts

The surgical cut was made with a butterknife after it had been slowly and patiently sharpened on the sandstone prison brick. More scalpel than shiv, it sliced through skin, stomach and then artery: the target of the attack.

Pffffft.

Blood spurted from the victim's belly, covering the attacker in red. The man with the weapon licked his lips. Then he growled.

He wasn't done yet.

Frederick Valdez Ford flicked his wrist and sent the shiv south. The movement was violent, full of anger and rage, but somehow delicate and precise at the same time. The blade sliced down, cutting vertically through Wanna Chamron's coeliac artery. He split the life-pumping highway as he swiped, then severed it horizontally with a sideways jerk, at the exact point where it divides into the legs.

Pffffft. Pause. *Pffffft.* Pause. *Pffffft.*

With each fading beat, Chamron's heart spat a small bucket of blood onto the yard.

Splat. Pause. *Splat.* Pause. *Splat.*

Chamron, 26, soon bled out. The cold concrete covered with claret, the Cambodian refugee was dead, his stay in Goulburn Jail lasting exactly 125 minutes.

Welcome to the Killing Fields – a place to kill or be killed. The suspected member of the 5T Asian crime gang was the first of seven inmates to be murdered at the prison in just two years – 11 months and one day – making Goulburn Jail the most murderous prison in Australia.

23 September 1995, 2.53pm . . . the killing begins.

Chamron nonchalantly walked from the bus. He spoke to no one and looked as if he didn't have a care in the world as he entered the reception room; the smell of stale piss was masked by buckets of bleach. He said nothing as a guard commanded, 'Spread your cheeks.' He was silent as he grabbed his greens and was overtly obliging as he was shoved into his cell.

Chamron had five months left to serve. He didn't care if he finished it in Goulburn or Guantanamo Bay. Soon he would be out, back to his drugs and dodgy deals.

He had behaved badly in Parramatta Jail and had been sent to Goulburn as punishment.

So what? I'm 5T. Nobody's gonna fuck with me.

It was this arrogant attitude that allowed him to be lured into the shower block just two hours after he arrived.

'Hey, I'll show you around,' said the man known as Freddy Ford. 'Come with me. You are one of us.'

Ford, a Filipino national, was heavily linked to Asian crime.

'This is Amoh,' he said, pointing at another inmate – Nico Norma Emery Amohanga, a 21-year-old New Zealander. 'You remember him, right?'

Chamron, who had arrived in Australia with his sister as a refugee in 1992, did know Amoh. He knew Freddy, too. The trio had been locked up together as kids at the Mount Penang Juvenile Justice Centre at Kariong, just north of Sydney.

Yard 3 was busy. Inmates from both B and C wings roamed free.

'Over here,' Ford said, leading Chamron towards the shower block.

'This way.' Chamron turned back to Amoh.

Whack. He was stabbed in the back.

'What the fuck?' Chamron demanded, blindsided by the sneaky shot.

Ford pulled the butterknife out and reloaded his arm.

Chamron turned into lightning, crashing into Amoh before doing the bolt. He screamed as he ran towards the Circle.

'I'm stabbed,' he cried. 'I'm fucking stabbed!'

But the yard was bustling, filled with noisy inmates on the move.

'Time to finish,' a guard shouted. 'Time for muster.'

Inmates spewed out of the shower block and were herded to a grassed area at the back of C Wing.

Chamron ran. But Ford ran faster, knife in hand and lackey a stride behind.

The fresh meat closed in on the gate. There were guards there. *They'll save me, right?*

Thud.

Amoh sprinted past Ford and downed Chamron with a haymaker to the chest. The victim desperately jumped off the concrete and regained his balance. He looked up and saw Ford.

That's when the butterknife-turned-scalpel delivered the blow and slashed through the vital artery in his stomach. Chamron clutched at the gaping hole in his guts and dropped. He would soon be dead.

'You fucking dog!' shouted Ford as he drove the knife through Chamron's eye and into his brain.

One final blow, just to be sure.

Goulburn Governor Allan Chisholm was sifting through reports when he was interrupted. He was almost through the paper pile.

'A murder, boss,' said the officer. 'A new bloke has been gutted.'

Chisholm pushed his chair back, grabbed a notepad and steeled himself for the fresh stack of reports that would surely follow. 'Here we go.'

The boss was new to Goulburn himself.

'I was the governor at Goulburn between 1993 and 1996,' Chisholm later recalled.

'And that was a famously difficult period down there. I had worked at plenty of jails: Parramatta, Muswellbrook, Grafton, Kirkconnell, Glen Innes and Long Bay. They were tough places, Grafton and Long Bay in particular, but they had nothing on Goulburn. My initial thoughts when I was told I was going to Goulburn were, *Well, you have got to be fucking joking.* There were rumours about the conduct of the staff, and the problems with inmates were well known.'

Ironically, going to the worst jail in the state was supposed to be a reward for being the best officer.

'In 1992 the commissioner rated the jails from worst to best,' Chisholm continued.

'One being the worst, two the second worst and so on. And then he rated the superintendents; one being the best and so on. So the guy rated number one went to the worst jail. Initially I was rated number three and was sent to Parramatta. That was fine with me. But the number one guy refused to take on Goulburn – and so did the number two guy when they came to him. I was ordered to take up the post, and the boss made it very clear to me that I could not refuse. So I ended up at Goulburn; the hardest bloody institution they had.

'I remember my first day there like it was yesterday. You could cut the air with a knife. There was so much tension in the place – it was that intense. I met the governor that I was taking over from, and he was a shattered man. He was spilling coffee, his hands shaking from stress. I looked at him and said, "What have I got myself in to."'

This would be the first of four murders Chisholm would investigate.

'Oh, there were stabbings every day,' Chisholm said. 'It's a miracle there weren't plenty more that ended up dead.'

Chamron's was the first murder he attended, and it officially began the murderous period at Goulburn that saw the prison dubbed the 'Killing Fields'.

'I was called down as soon as they found this guy,' Chisholm said. 'There are procedures to be put in place, like preserving the crime scene and filling out the crime scene logs of who enters it and when. You have to be quick. Being the governor of the institution, I also had to identify the inmate that had been killed. I was also responsible for interviewing the person I suspected of the murder.'

Chisholm deduced that the dead man, the one with his guts now lying all over the concrete floor, knew his attackers. He was not a random inmate targeted as soon as he jumped off the bus.

'It had to be about a drug deal,' Chisholm said. 'A carry-over from another prison. These guys knew he was coming here and I reckon they had been ordered to put a hit on him. This one all revolved around that Vietnamese gang – the 5T. He was killed by one of them. He went through reception and Freddy Ford met him and walked him across to the shower. He did him there. Ford was doing life and was a gang member. He had Filipino in him, and boy did he know what he was doing. I remember being astounded by the way Chamron died and that Ford was such an expert killer.'

Ford was also an expert in the art of silence.

'He looked me straight in the face and said, "If I did do it and you prove it, what are you going to do? Give me life?"' Chisholm recalled. 'He was just belligerent. He wouldn't admit to anything, but he didn't care if he was charged and convicted all the same.'

Ian Norris was one of the officers ordering the prisoners from the shower block when Chamron was murdered. He gave a statement to the police, offering a chilling comment on how such a grisly crime could happen so openly . . . without anyone witnessing or knowing a thing.

NSW Police

STATEMENT in the matter of: Murder of Wanna Chamron. 25 September 1995.

15. At approximately 2.55pm on Saturday 23 September 1995, First Class Prison Officer Martin and I were supervising the clearing of the shower block in the preparation for the afternoon muster. We call out, 'Time to finish. Time for muster.' We watch the inmates leave the shower block and open the connecting gate to allow them into the grassed area at the back of C Wing. The shower block is locked.

16. At this time which was approximately 2.55pm, I received some information via the portable radio that I was carrying. As a result of this information I had a conversation with First Class Prison Officer Martin. We

both remained in the grassed area and started locking the inmates that had been in 3 Yard back into 6 Yard adjacent to the kitchen. By doing this 6 Yard became crowded with approximately 40 inmates.

17. At approximately 3.20pm, First Class Prison Officer Martin and I walked through C Wing, to the Centre Circle. I remained in the Centre Circle for approximately 3 minutes. I saw that Ambulance Officers were on the scene, at the front of gate 3. The Ambulance Officers were on the Circle side of the gate of 3 Yard. I saw that they were treating an inmate now known to me as Wanna Chamron.

18. I saw that Wanna Chamron was lying on his back. He was wearing prison-issue greens. I saw blood on his chest area and head. There was also a large amount of blood on the concrete ground, around his body. There was a large number of Prison Officers in the area watching the proceedings.

20. The first time that I saw Chamron was when he was lying on the ground in the Circle. I deal with many prisoners every day. They are always coming and going. I do get to recognise some of them. I was not familiar with Chamron in any way. I did not recognise him in 3 Yard at any time. I did not recognise this inmate on the occasions that I was escorting inmates from 3 Yard into the shower block.

I do not know how this person received his injuries, and I do not know how he came to be lying in the position when I first saw him on Saturday afternoon at approximately 3.20pm.

Norris knew much more about the next murder. It still gives him nightmares . . .

Holey Horror

'He ran out bleeding like a stuck pig,' said Norris. 'He was running towards us, saying, "Gate up, chief. Gate up!" He was covered in blood and began stumbling. And then he fell.'

Norris rushed over and dropped next to the prisoner, his knees landing in a quickly expanding puddle of blood.

'I looked down at his torso and there were holes everywhere,' Norris said. 'I started sticking my fingers into his wounds to try and stop the bleeding. One . . . two . . . Eventually I had every finger in a stab hole. I had no more fingers and he had plenty more holes, so there was nothing more I could do. I screamed for help as I was sprayed with blood. I was absolutely covered from head to toe. He was pushing other officers and me away as we tried to keep him still and lying down. I heard him mumble something, but I couldn't make out what it was.'

Maurice Joseph Marsland, 35, was a rapist, a predator and a rock spider (a prison term for a child sex offender). Despised and reviled, he was serving a 12-year sentence for multiple sexual assaults. The media called him the Eastern Suburbs Rapist. Prison officers called him a piece of shit.

'Marsland was a well-known predator,' said former Governor Chisholm. 'A sexual predator. He was a rapist on the outside and a rapist on the inside. He was a huge Aboriginal bloke, real big and real intimidating. And he could be a real arsehole. Generally he stuck to himself, but from time to time he was involved in skirmishes. He might steal someone else's piece of arse and someone would go after him, or something like that. But it usually didn't end well for the people who went after him, because he could fight.

'He was certainly a target but he never asked for protection because he figured he could protect himself. He walked around doing what he wanted and taking what he wanted. He was a real piece of shit.'

Marsland had been attacked in the shower.

Whack.

He hadn't even had a chance to take off his shoes.

Whack. Whack.

He took a swing, slapping nothing but air.

Whack. Whack. Whack.

He desperately grabbed one of his attackers.

Whack. Whack. Whack. Whack.

The blows kept coming. He was stabbed relentlessly. The weapon: a piece of reinforcement building steel.

Whaooof.

The giant of a man pushed with all his might and two of his attackers hit the floor. And then the rapist ran – out of the shower block, towards the guards at the gate.

'Gate up, chief. Gate up!'

Norris recalled the crime scene: 'There wasn't as much blood in the showers as you would have thought. He obviously wasn't attacked while he was showering because he was fully clothed. They most likely ambushed him when he came in. He came out with his shorts and shirt on. I think I was the one that ripped his shirt off when I was trying to get to all his wounds.'

Marsland's assault occurred on 13 February 1996, less than five months after Chamron's stabbing death. Marsland had been running towards the same gate that the 5T gang member never got to, screaming as he grabbed at his bloody wounds.

He dropped and, despite Norris's efforts, died.

'Marsland died on the Circle, as far as I was concerned,' Norris said. 'There were two versions: one with him dying there and one with him dying at the hospital. But looking at his body, looking at his wounds, I'm pretty sure he died in my arms.'

Chisholm was fast on the scene.

'He bled out in the yard,' the governor confirmed. 'And he died before he was loaded into the back of the ambulance.'

Chisholm fingered three men for the murder.

'One of them was a guy who was doing a triple life sentence for another murder,' said Chisholm. 'And from what I can work out, Marsland was killed as payback for something that had happened in Lithgow Jail. It was a frenzied attack and he ended up with 34 stab wounds. The killing blow was concluded to be the one he copped in the throat. One of the shivs was a long piece of steel and it just ripped his throat apart. We were doing construction around the jail at the time of the murders, and the prisoners were getting their hands on building materials.'

Chisholm suspects Marsland was lured into the shower block under false pretenses.

'Maybe they said they had a bloke in there for him to rape,' Chisholm said. 'And what happened next was just brutal. They really got into him and it was over in seconds. What you have to remember about jail fights is that they are real quick. They have a small window to attack and they go for maximum damage. It was a frantic job, and we found out that one of the killers got so excited while attacking [Marsland] that he pissed himself. Apparently Marsland had bashed and raped someone in Lithgow. Maybe he took someone's piece of arse. Anyway, there was some big blue at Lithgow and a hit was put on him.'

The shower block is notorious for stabbings.

'All the officers had complained about the shower block in that wing for years,' Norris said. 'It should not have been built. Those showers were a very, very dangerous place to be. The officers have almost no vision into them, and under the privacy laws there can be no cameras. There were no guards inside, but there always had to be a guard standing outside. But one guard by himself is useless – all a crim has to do is distract him. That could be as easily done as asking him to go and get a block of soap. You had to walk at least 20 metres away to get the soap, and by the time you came back there could be a dead guy lying in the showers. The staffing in the jails is horribly low. When I was there you were looking at a ratio of 50 inmates to one guard. It's worse now – about 75 to one.'

*

30

The three men suspected of Marsland's murder were detained and the investigation began.

'The jail was sealed up for almost a week,' Norris said. 'They went around with a squad, searching for the shivs. They searched up and down the gutters, inside the cells and everywhere in the yard. I think they did find one, but they could never prove that it was the weapon that killed Marsland. Inmates are experts at hiding shivs. They hide them in the gutters, in the roofing, in steel tube railings that they even find a way to weld shut. They will even put it in a plastic bag and shove it up their backsides.'

Norris became a vital witness as police began to build their case, offering up his personal notes from the day of the attack and providing a statement where he identified bank robber Raymond Carrion as suspect no.1.

'The first time I saw Marsland he was on his knees near the front gate and facing away from the gate. I was 15 feet away from Marsland and had a good view of him. I could see his back. As I ran towards the gate I saw an inmate known to me as Raymond Carrion.

'Raymond Carrion was standing to the left of, and slightly behind, Marsland. I saw Carrion raise his right hand with a clenched fist above Marsland's head. I saw Carrion move his clenched fist in a downward motion. I saw Carrion's clenched fist strike Marsland in the head. Carrion repeated this motion. The hits were in quick succession. Carrion again used his right clenched fist to strike Marsland on the right shoulder.

'I saw Carrion run straight down the yard. I don't know

where he got to. By the time I got to the gate, Raymond Carrion was out of sight.'

The police statement, dated 13 February 1996, also details Norris's frantic bid to save Marsland's life.

18. Prison Officer Brownlie and I placed Marsland on his left side in an attempt to slow down the blood that was coming from the lower area of the front of his neck. I know that another Prison Officer, assisted by an inmate known to me as Alex Ibrahim, helped me take off Marsland's jail green T-shirt. I could see a number of small-type puncture wounds on Marsland's back in various positions. I saw blood coming from these puncture holes in Marsden's upper back.

19. I saw a member of the medical staff attend to Marsland and place a pad on Marsland's neck. The medical officer applied pressure to the pad. At this time Marsland was pushing other officers and me away from him as we tried to keep him still and lying down. I heard Marsland mumble something but I couldn't make out what it was.

Norris has no doubt Carrion killed Marsland.

'I was on the Circle and I started taking notes of everything that I saw. But I made a stupid mistake in crossing Carrion off my notes before putting him back on. I wasn't at first one hundred per cent sure that it was Carrion I saw hitting Marsland. He had come out of the showers with what looked like blood all over him. But he quickly went and got changed and came back wearing a clean shirt. That put some doubt in my mind.

'But then when I had a second look I absolutely knew it was him. The cops pulled me up on it because I'd crossed his name off that first list; they told me that that would ruin us in court. It made me look like I was a bit unsure, but I was completely sure.'

Chisholm interviewed Carrion following the attack. 'He just laughed and said, "Go on, put me in jail why don't you." That's the problem with these blokes. A lot of them have been jailed for life, so killing someone is nothing for them. They can't be punished further.'

Or so Carrion thought.

While awaiting trial for Marsland's murder, Carrion was found dead – his eyes stabbed out, his body fully bled. He was also killed in the shower.

'That was payback for Marsland,' Chisholm said.

Marsland has been dead for almost 20 years, but Norris sees him on most nights.

'He is there,' Norris said. 'In my dreams. In my night-mares. I suffer from post-traumatic stress disorder, and he haunts me when I sleep. I can see him there . . . dying in my arms.'

Norris feared he had contracted HIV following the murder when Marsland was found to have full-blown AIDS.

'It was a living hell,' Norris said. 'I had to wait a long time to get the test results back and I thought I was done. He had bled all over me and I had been sticking my fingers straight into his wounds. I found out I was okay, but I was still really miserable for the next five years. I am better now, but I still suffer from it. I see him in my dreams, and no one should ever have to go through something like that.'

Unfortunately, plenty at Goulburn did.

White Powder and White Ox

He nodded at his partner after winning the trick. 'My luck is with me today,' he said. He looked back at his cards, all neatly sorted: blacks with blacks, reds with reds, spades next to clubs, diamonds hanging out alongside hearts. 'Your turn.'

The inmate next to him also had his cards precisely fanned. Mr My-Turn-Next reached out to pluck a card. But then he stopped, his gaze suddenly frozen on Mr Lucky-One-Who-Won-The-Trick. Well, not *on* him . . . behind him.

Shhliiiiiit.

Serrated steel flashed across flesh, a lightning wrist action slashing open the card player's neck.

'Eerrrr. Eerrrr,' the victim rattled. His hands flew towards his throat, throwing cards and then finding blood.

Whack. Whack.

Lightning struck twice, then three times, four, the slicing motion now a stabbing one – the target the body, not the throat. The other men at the table remained still. Remained silent. And they never *would* talk, the full story of the Colombian cocaine king's killing remaining a mystery. Until now . . .

*

A former Elizabeth Bay waiter, Javier Francisco Lara-Gomez was arrested in 1993 after being busted with 98kg of cocaine – the biggest ever seizure in Australia – and sentenced to 18 years in jail. Known as 'Frank', his case intrigued the nation: A Colombian in Sydney? A Colombian in Sydney with 98kg of Colombian cocaine?

He was our own Pablo Escobar: all Medellín, machine guns and millions stacked neatly in brief cases. It was reported that Lara-Gomez, just months before his death, had given a statement to the Corrective Services Internal Investigations Unit, claiming he had paid a criminal network $350,000 to bust him from Parramatta Jail. He was also constantly being pursued by organised crime investigators wanting the details of his knowledge of the cartels. Lara-Gomez was allegedly being offered a chance to return to his homeland to complete his sentence in return for giving information to the Australian Federal Police.

Bottom line: Lara-Gomez didn't talk to anyone. He knew the cartel he was dealing with, and he knew what breaking the strict code of silence meant – death. He refused to talk to Australian Federal Police after his arrest in 1993, and he also declined to give evidence at his trial. Lara-Gomez was resigned, even content, to do his time. He made the most of prison life. He was regarded as a model inmate while at Sydney's Long Bay Jail. He painted, sculpted clay and kept himself out of harm's way. And then he was moved to Goulburn . . .

*

'No one dies in here,' Lara-Gomez said. 'Not in my wing. Not while I am in here.'

The Colombian was already a leader.

'What's it got to do with you?' the inmate said. 'Why do you care who we hit? There is a contract out on him.'

'I'm the sweeper,' Lara-Gomez replied, referring to the prison term for inmates who are given extra privileges in return for keeping order in a wing. 'And this wing is my responsibility. It's good in here now. We don't want that to change. Why bring trouble? The screws will come down on me and make life tough for everyone.'

The wannabe contract killer turned his back and walked away. He was fuming. *Fucker thinks he can push us around. Big-shot Colombian. Fuck him and fuck his connections.* He stormed into the yard and put out a contract of his own: one packet of White Ox smokes for anyone who kills that son of a bitch Lara-Gomez.

'[Lara-Gomez] had actually stopped a hit earlier that day,' revealed former Goulburn Night Senior Kevin Camberwell. 'Being a Colombian, he was one of the blokes in charge of the yard. Nothing happened in the yard without his say-so. A couple of Aboriginals wanted to stab some other fella, and he stepped up and said, "That isn't happening in my yard."'

Camberwell, who worked in the wing where the murder took place, dismissed speculation that the murder was related to Lara-Gomez's drugs charge: 'It wasn't over drugs or anything like that. Not at all. He was just a victim of Goulburn. A contract was put on him, a packet of White Ox the payment, and inmate Ronald Priestly took it up. He was the one who killed him, and a bloke named Carl Little was the one who ordered the hit.'

Camberwell said the Indigenous inmates were particularly volatile because of a perceived lack of power within the jail. No Aboriginal inmate had held the position of prison sweeper, and they were pissed off about it, especially since Lara-Gomez had been handed the privilege almost as soon as he arrived.

'The Aboriginals didn't like being told what to do in any case,' Camberwell said, 'and it was just a power show. Like in most places, the Aboriginals had no pull in the yard – even though they outnumbered everyone else.'

Priestly, a notorious inmate who would soon spark a prison riot before being moved to Supermax, waited for his moment. And he did not have to wait too long. Lara-Gomez was easy meat, the drug-dealing prison sweeper sitting down for a game of cards following lunch. Lara-Gomez was facing a wall. He wouldn't see it coming.

Armed with a large knife, Priestly crept up behind Lara-Gomez, slit his throat and stabbed him another 26 times. He must have really wanted those cigarettes.

'It was a gruesome killing,' Camberwell recalled. 'It was actually in my wing at the time: C Wing, 7 Yard. He never saw it coming. He was sitting under the shelter, playing away, and then he was dead.'

Camberwell recalled eating pizza over Lara-Gomez's corpse after the killing:

'I was actually the one who had to guard the body. We called it "body watch", and I was keeping the crows from pecking at him. I was standing there eating pizza when the coppers arrived, and they asked me how I could stomach it. I just laughed and said, "Easy, I'm hungry." I was there for a few hours waiting for the coroner, standing over the dead body.'

The autopsy concluded that the weapon used in the killing was a hunting knife. The revelation astounded guards and fuelled the conspiracy theories.

'Most inmates are stabbed with shivs,' said a guard who asked to remain unnamed. 'Sharpened toothbrushes, bedsprings, bits of metal they pull out of buckets. But this bloke was killed with a knife. And not just a knife, a friggin' huge hunting knife. That is not something that would be easy to get into a prison, or to hide. We will never know where it came from.'

Police were at a loss when it came to finding the hunting knife or the killer.

'We didn't see a thing,' all the prisoners said. 'Don't know nothing.'

There was no video footage. No suspects. No obvious motive for anyone in the wing to have killed him.

Must have been them Colombians.

The 'long and vengeful arm of the Central American drug cartel' was first blamed for the execution. And why not? Surely the people who gave Lara-Gomez the 98kg of cocaine were mad. Maybe they were even murderous, considering he had been offered the prospect of parole in return for evidence.

The incident was initially reported as a 'symbolic slaying, a grisly warning to all foot soldiers in the Medellín Cartel that their silence is absolute'.

'Then the weapon was found,' Camberwell said. 'It wasn't found for a couple of years, but it was found all the same. A random search stumbled upon a hunting knife, and they knew straightaway what it was and who it had been used on. It was found in the S-bend of a toilet in the yard. And that's when they found the killer . . . not a Colombian, but a bloke who was killing for a smoke.'

'Priestly only put up his hand when the weapon was found, because he knew his fingerprints were on it,' Camberwell continued. 'He would have been pinched anyway, but when they found [the knife] I think he *wanted* to be pinched because he was a dead man walking if he ever left the jail. . . . The Colombians were waiting for him to be released. He wanted to make sure he was in a place like Supermax where they couldn't get at him.'

So, despite suggestions of cartels, corruption and cocaine-crazed Colombians, Lara-Gomez turned out to be just another victim in the Killing Fields.

Mr Singh?

Pritam Singh walked into Goulburn Jail's voluminous reception room.

'I shouldn't be here,' Singh, a rapist, said to a fellow prisoner. 'I've been sent to a prison farm in Tumbarumba. You know? A low-security joint. But apparently the five-hour trip from Sydney can't be done in a day, so I have to spend a night in here. In fucking Goulburn.'

Next.

'Spread your checks,' the guard yelled. 'Touch your toes.'

Singh reluctantly went through the obligatory search. He was stripped, showered and sent straight into the Killing Fields. Standing by himself, he looked at all the concrete and sandstone, wire and steel.

Sure it's intimidating, but no more than Long Bay, right?

His thoughts were interrupted.

'You Singh?' a man asked, seemingly popping up from nowhere.

The rapist replied that he was.

'Excuse me,' the man said. 'What did you say?'

The now curious Singh again replied in the affirmative.

'Are you SINGH?' This time the man was louder and more forceful.

'Yeah, I'm Singh.' He nodded a third time. 'That's me.'

Those were the last words Singh ever said. The inquiring inmate, who was concealing a shiv in his right hand, unleashed, sending the sharpened steal into flesh.

Pop. Pop. Pop.

The blade tore holes in Singh's torso, the 36-year-old folding his arms across his chest in a futile bid to shield himself from the blows.

The attacker adjusted his aim.

Pop.

The shiv took out Singh's eye.

The Malaysian national was soon dead, the brutal attack over in ten seconds. The killer walked back into the wing.

Hours passed. Singh's body was bagged and tagged, his night's stay in Goulburn cut short.

'Time to pay up,' the killer demanded later, standing toe-to-toe with the man who had ordered the hit. 'I killed him and now I'm here to collect.'

The other inmate laughed. 'You ain't getting a thing, mate – you got the wrong Singh!'

The killer turned white.

'That fella was a case of mistaken identity,' Camberwell later revealed. 'His murder was a mistake. There was a contract out on an inmate with the same last name and he also had a very similar first name.'

Few felt sorry for Singh. The murdered man was part of a trio who had kidnapped and raped a 29-year-old woman in a sickening attack that was recorded on a video camera. Singh and another man, Biswaseet Singh, had grabbed the woman and took her into her Dulwich Hill home in Sydney and tied her to a bed. They then sexually assaulted her as a third man filmed the attack. The woman's horror was not over following the assault. Singh and his gang held her captive until she agreed to pay them $1500 cash and sign over her car.

Singh's immediate family was in the minority when it came to being outraged by his killing at Goulburn.

'Why was he out in the yard mixing with the heaviest

criminals when he was only a minimum-security prisoner?' asked an uncle.

The killer was left angry and humiliated. He was not paid for the hit, having mixed up his Singhs.

'They get information about the new arrivals,' said a guard who asked to be unnamed. 'Just through the jail grapevine. They know who's coming in and whether or not there is a contract out on them.'

Kevin Camberwell said inmates were willing killers for hire; they had so little to lose. 'It didn't matter how big the payout was because most of the blokes who would do it were already in for life. They couldn't serve any *more* than life. They would wait around in the yard when they knew someone was coming in and just walk up to people and ask them their names. If they said a name that was on a contract, they would kill them there and then.'

And that's what happened to Singh.

The killer was never identified. At least not officially.

'Most of the killings ... nobody was stung for them,' said Camberwell. 'We knew who [murdered Singh], and we had the cameras there, but it couldn't be proved. The cameras did not show enough to identify anyone, and no one would talk.'

The officers did know enough to have a laugh. Not about the killing, of course, but over the killer not getting paid.

'He was just lucky the guy he got was a rapist – or he may have ended up with a contract of his own,' a guard said.

Boots and Blankets

Night Senior Camberwell cracked open the gate and entered the yard.

'G'day, chief,' said the inmate as the Goulburn veteran watched the gate swing shut.

Camberwell nodded. 7 Yard was a heaving sea of prison green – inmates buzzing back and forth, a group of men laughing, another in a play fight.

'I was coming back through the yard,' the guard later recalled. 'I usually worked in this particular wing, but for some reason I was doing a shift in activities on that day. I had just finished. Nothing unusual going on. Just another Monday, the yard packed for lunch.'

Eyes forward, shoulders back, Camberwell walked purposefully through the yard. He was not in the mood for conversation, and a nod of his head was the only acknowledgement the prisoners were going to get. The officer's mechanical march was suddenly broken.

'I just hopped for a moment,' the officer said. 'A big step, not a jump.'

The officer looked back at what caused him to break stride. It was a blanket lying in the yard. Camberwell had stepped right over it. *Oh well. Whatever.* He turned his head and continued along.

'Then I thought, *That's not right.* So I stopped and took another look at the blanket.' *So what? Just another blanket dumped in the yard.* Then he saw the boots.

'There were two boots at the end of the blanket,' Camberwell continued. 'Two prison-issue desert boots, the toes

43

pointing straight towards the sky.' The officer retraced his steps. 'I pulled up the blanket and a dead man was lying there. White as a ghost, except for all the blood.'

Camberwell knew who the body belonged to, even before he reefed the rug and looked death in the face.

'There was a brown type of desert boot they could get,' Camberwell said. 'But there was only one bloke in the entire jail who wore them. His name was Henry, Terence Henry, and he was a bit of a nothing, really.'

So the blanket came off and the bled-out body did indeed belong to Henry.

'There was blood everywhere,' Camberwell said. 'I pulled the blanket back. There was no need to attempt CPR or anything like that because he was long gone. All I could do was raise the alarm. I alerted the rest of the staff and they called the emergency muster.'

It turns out Camberwell wasn't the only one who had stepped over the body.

'He had been lying there for a number of hours,' Camberwell said. 'They had murdered him before lunch and just left him there, covered with a blanket. People either didn't notice or didn't care. The crims had been walking over him for hours like he didn't exist.'

Henry had been at Goulburn for just four days. Slapped with a minor sentence for break, enter and steal, resisting arrest and common assault, he lasted less than 100 hours in Australia's most murderous jail.

'He got knocked for being an arsehole,' said Camberwell. 'He was a nobody that wanted to be someone. He walked into the jail acting like a big man, acting all tough.'

Allegedly a standover man in other New South Wales prisons, Henry demanded respect. He got death instead.

'He pissed off the wrong people and they were quickly fed up with him,' Camberwell said of the 22-year-old. 'He was just a young bloke in way over his head.'

Henry's murder remains unsolved – the latest victim of the Killing Fields. Once again, 7 Yard.

'You couldn't identify who killed him because there were so many around,' Camberwell said. 'The inmates just ignore shit like that. They don't want to make it their business, and this bloke had no friends. He would have lain there a lot longer had I not literally stepped over his body. He would have been there until the yard was emptied and muster done.'

Henry was Goulburn's seventh murder in just over two years, killed on 24 August 1998.

John Coffey 2.0

Allan Chisholm was the boss of Goulburn Jail during the height of the Killing Fields period – the most murderous time in Australian penal history. He was the Goulburn Governor who had to lift back the sheet and look into the eyes of four of the seven murdered men.

Chisholm had heard Maurice Marsland take his last breath: the wheezing rattle that whispered from his bloodied, bruised and brutally ripped apart breast, followed by a splatter of blood that landed on the governor's wrist. He had helped paramedics load the dead rapist into the back of a truck.

Chisholm was also the man who had pulled Wanna

Chamron's prison file from a drawer, walked it to his body and then matched the mugshot to the dead face. He'd then stood beside the body, waiting for the police to come, his vision full of intestine as he shooed away insects attempting to infect the pile of innards.

'Yep,' he said. 'I was called down for all of them. I had to look at all the bodies, because I was the one who had to identify them. I couldn't leave the body until the police or coroner arrived. I had to make sure no one messed with the body, removed any evidence or walked over fingerprints.

'I can remember on one morning we had five stabbings. They didn't die, but it was only because of luck, and the quick-thinking reaction from officers. And then there were the bashings. Don't even bother asking how many because I can't count that high.

'There were also assaults on guards. It was a very dangerous place. A very, very dangerous place. But it was best known for the bodies, and I saw all of them.'

So I asked Chisholm about the nightmares, about the mental scars. Which one of these deaths – the bodies, the blood and the post-mortem bruising – affected him the most?

'None of them, to be honest,' Chisholm replied. 'Sure, it does affect you – watching a man die is not pleasant – but with all of them . . . well . . . it was just part of the job. But there was a particular death during my time at Goulburn that stands out. One that really got to me and one that I am still saddened by now.'

You didn't have to be *killed* to be claimed by the Killing Fields . . .

*

'Hey you, retard,' the inmate yelled, throwing a handful of food slop.

Whack.

'Yeah you, dumb shit,' he continued to bully as the leftover meat and veggies slid down the target's spine. 'You giant piece of spastic shit. I'm going to hurt you. Hurt you real bad.'

Backed by a posse of tattooed arms and battle-scarred heads, the big-mouthed man stepped in.

Crack.

His leading left crashed into chin.

Smash.

His right, the enforcer's trusted knock-out blow, slammed into temple.

The 'giant piece of spastic shit' shook his head. 'Don't make me hurt you,' he said. 'I don't want to have to hurt you. No trouble, please.'

The prison heavy went red with rage.

Thud.

A body shot this time. *Maybe the fat fuck likes being hit in his gluttonous gut?*

Wrong.

The giant wrapped his hands around the attacker's neck, and with nothing more than a flick of his wrists and a shoulder twitch, he lifted the prisoner into the air.

'I told you!' the giant screamed.

Crrrrrrack!

The force of the blow that followed knocked the name-calling, food-throwing man out cold.

'He never hurt anyone unless he had to,' recalled Chisholm of Robert Steele, a man imprisoned for his role in five murders.

'Only once that I can recall. He was a bit like the guy [John Coffey] from the movie *The Green Mile* – a gentle giant who looked like a killer. He was simple but kind, and could have destroyed anyone in the jail but didn't. He was that sort of inmate. I really had a soft spot for him, and I don't think he should have even been in jail.'

March, 1993.

The rays of the rising summer sun, hot enough to wring steam from the damp grass, could not drive the evil away.

The light did not deter the devil.

'I ain't going out without a fight,' said self-described socio-path Leonard Leabeater, surrounded by police in a Hanging Rock Station farmhouse at Cangai, New South Wales. 'I'm going to make sure they kill me.'

He hugged the shotgun like a teddy bear as he reflected on the two hostages he had just released: Trevor Lasserre, 11, and his sister Tonia, 6.

'I don't kill people under 12,' he boasted. 'I'd rather be in South Australia killing cops.'

Leabeater had let the children go shortly after fellow fugitive Raymond Bassett surrendered himself to police; the 25-year-old wasn't ready to die. The third murderer, Robert Steele, 22, stayed with Leabeater even after the children had been released. Like Bassett, he didn't want to be shot down in a hail of bullets, but he couldn't leave the man who had taken him in, either. Steele believed Leabeater was the religious prophet of the spirit Astra. He had followed Leabeater, who foretold that his own death would come when he was killed by a warlock, without question. But with the death he predicted drawing near – it would later be revealed he told his sister he would die on an altar on the fourth month of 1993 – Leabeater instructed his loyal follower to leave. He told him to walk towards the light.

At 6am Steele strolled from the farmhouse, calmly smoking a Winfield Red, and handed himself over to police.

But Leabeater remained in the dark. The fresh sun, the threatening guns and the pleas driven through police-issue PAs not stopping him from claiming one last life – his own.

After a 26-hour siege, the nine-day rampage that saw Leabeater, Bassett and Steele kill five people was finally over. Leabeater's body was found lying on a blood-soaked bed, a half-smoked cigarette still gripped between his fingers. A shotgun was lying next to the remains of his head.

Bassett and Steele were charged with the murders of a pregnant 14-year-old, whose charred remains were found on a Queensland farm; three miners, all shot in the head and two thrown from a cliff; and a helicopter mechanic murdered near Mount Isa.

Bassett was given two life sentences for the shocking crime. Steele received five life sentences plus 12 years without the possibility of parole.

The giant Steele, 130kg of bulk and brawn, was sent to Goulburn Jail. That's where he pulled out a packet of Winfield Reds and offered it to the boss.

'I smoked Marlboros, and he looked at them and told me they were no good,' recalled Chisholm. 'He offered me his whole pack. I remember that because no one in prison had ever offered me anything, and smokes were a very big deal to them. They are like gold in prison. That was the first time I saw his good heart.'

The next time Chisholm saw the giant's kindness was when he reluctantly flayed the bully.

'A crook was picking on him,' Chisholm said. 'He was a heavy and he was giving Steele heaps because he was simple. The guy was in high-security because he was a handful; someone who couldn't be contained elsewhere. He was a tough bloke, but he picked out Steele. It was a huge mistake. Steele upended him and knocked him out with a single blow. He could have kept on going, but he walked away. He didn't hurt him more than he had to, and I was there soon after the fight. He was apologising. "It's not my fault, chief," he said. "He was picking on me. I'm sorry, *sorry, sorry, SORRY*. I didn't mean to hurt him so bad."'

Chisholm knew Steele was telling the truth. 'He could have killed the bloke if he wanted to – and everyone else in the room – with his bare hands. But he was just protecting himself.'

Chisholm found Steele to be incredibly kind but easily led.

'He was involved in that hostage thing,' Chisholm said. 'He was involved in the killings and the siege, but it was a cult-type thing and he was very young. I'll go further than that – to be blunt, he was retarded. He wasn't all there. He was the youngest, and he was taken advantage of. He was like a big kid who is extremely strong. He believed in what the other two were doing and he did as he was told.'

Chisholm became fascinated with the behemoth man-child.

'I was always in close contact with Steele,' Chisholm said. 'And I built a rapport with him, mainly because we initially thought he was going to be such a threat to everyone else in the jail and a major problem. But he didn't hurt officers or anyone else. I would tell him to get back to his cell and he did.

'I honestly believe he should not have been in jail,' Chisholm continued.

'He should have been in some psychiatric facility. He was a child trapped in a giant's body. Yes, he deserved to be punished because of his horrendous crimes, and he couldn't live in society, but Goulburn wasn't the place for him, and it would kill him.'

Chisholm got the call on Christmas Eve, 1994.

'He's dead, boss,' said an officer. 'You better come down.'

Steele was on his knees, a twisted blanket the only thing stopping his head from falling onto the cell floor.

'About 12.05am we got a call to say he had necked himself,' Chisholm said. 'He was so big that he had to kneel down and fall forward to get enough tension on the sheet. He had tied it to the cell bars and pulled forward until he was dead. It took us ages just to get him out of the cell because he was so big. It was really a horrible thing to see.'

Steele was to spend Christmas in solitary confinement after threatening to go out with a bang.

'I went and saw him on that Christmas Eve because of some allegations he had made,' Chisholm recalled. 'He always said that he was going to go out with something big and that he was going to make headlines. He said he would take officers with him, and that he would do it on Christmas Day. We didn't think he would harm anyone, but we had to take the threat seriously. He could have caused absolute havoc in the prison. We would not have been able to handle him. It would have taken lots of men to contain him, and there would have been a lot hurt.

'So we put him in segregation for the night. We told him no officer was going to go near him because of what he had said. We told him no officer would come, even if he knocked. They would have to call me first, and I would come and see him. He assured me there would be no problem. He seemed absolutely normal.'

The next time Chisholm would see Steele, the prisoner would be dead.

'It was a complete shock,' he said. 'We had no idea he would hurt himself. We were worried about others, not him. It's the prison death that has affected me the most. It was such a sad tale, and I still think about it now.'

Why?

Former prison officer Dave Farrell attempted to explain Goulburn Jail's unprecedented deaths:

'I picked up the command in Goulburn in 1996, and all the killings were just happening when I arrived. I was in charge of the whole region as a commander. It was just a bad mix of prisoners with conflicts that intel didn't know about. They were out to kill their enemies if they had the chance – and some of them did. It was all internal politics among the criminals. Some of them didn't have the intention to use the shiv; they would arm themselves for protection. But if they got the opportunity, then they would also use it to attack.

'It was very rare to have all those killings at once, but it was a case of having all the shit in one place at one time – blokes who didn't blink at murdering someone else.'

Pain in the Arse

'Ahhhhh! AHHHHH!'

The painful scream broke the night's silence, the raw terror bouncing off the concrete and escaping through the bars.

'Help me, for fuck's sake! Someone FUCKING HELP ME!'

Inmates sprung from their beds; some were concerned for the man in pain.

'Chief,' one yelled. 'Chief, quick, I think someone's getting 'emselves killed!'

Others were more worried about their sleep: 'Shut the fuck up, or I'll give you something that *really* hurts!'

The wing was soon thundering, the noise summonsing the reluctant night guard.

'Boss, you better come take a look at this,' said the night supervisor over the phone.

Governor Chisholm walked into the cell.

'Oh shit,' he said, looking at all the blood. The inmate was naked from the waist down, and blood was coming from his anus. 'What the hell do we have here?'

The inmate, still in extraordinary pain, attempted to explain to the boss why he wasn't wearing pants and why he had blood gushing from his arse.

'Ah, fuck,' he said. 'Fuck. Fuck. Ah, I was getting up to have a piss and I – ah fuck, fuck, ah fuck, it hurts – and I slipped and something on the bed ripped open my arse.'

Chisholm looked at the bed. It was all blankets and mattress. For obvious reasons, there were no sharp bits, jutting metal or inmate-impaling poles.

'Oh, really?' Chisholm asked. 'You slipped and the mattress went up your arse?'

'Ah!' the inmate screamed. 'Ah. Yeah. Na. Fucked if I know. It just happened. Look at me – do you think I would do this to myself?'

Chisholm shrugged his shoulders. 'Well, not on purpose. I reckon you may have gone looking for something that we've been trying to find all day. Did you get it out?'

'There had been a stabbing earlier in the day,' Chisholm recalled. 'It could have very easily been another death in the

54

Killing Fields. It wasn't with what you would call a small shiv, and we thought it would be pretty easy to find. You really need to find the shiv or it makes it very difficult to nail someone for a stabbing in the yard. There are just too many people around for the officers to see it, and the cameras can't pick it up. It's not like out on the street where you would have witnesses come forward. Crims have a code of silence.'

The search, a thorough one at that, failed to find the weapon.

'It had vanished,' Chisholm continued. 'It wasn't in the yard, which was locked down as soon as it happened. We couldn't work out where it could have gone.'

It wasn't in the drains. Not in the gutters. Not in the rubbish bins.

'We had no idea until later that night,' Chisholm said, 'when we walked into the cell and saw all the blood.'

Yep, that's right – the prison yard attacker had hidden a piece of serrated steel up his arse. He had then gone to muster, ate dinner, had a shower and watched some TV, all the while with the shiv lodged in his rectum.

'That night he decided he needed to get it out,' Chisholm said. 'But the idiot had put it up there the wrong way. He had shoved it up blade-first and sliced his arse open when he stuck his fingers in to take it out.'

Chisholm did not buy the falling-on-the-bed-and-cutting-the-inside-of-my-arse story for a moment.

'We knew what had really happened,' Chisholm said. 'It was obvious. He refused to tell us and we said the doctor would not be able to treat him properly unless he came clean.

55

We said the doctor would not look for internal bleeding if he gave him the slipping story.'

The inmate soon produced a blade, big and bloody.

'He was a brave man putting it up there,' Chisholm said. 'A real shame for him that he did it for nothing and was caught red-handed, so to speak.'

Soon the deaths in the Killing Fields stopped, however. And it was all thanks to an accidental apartheid . . .

3

APARTHEID

The Potato Protest

'Nup,' barked the Aboriginal inmate. 'Not eating. Take it back. I'll eat it when it's brought to me by one of me own. I'd rather starve than take anything from another whitefella.'

And so the seed of an idea was sewn that would eventually be slammed as an apartheid . . .

Night senior Kevin Camberwell confronted the prison superintendent. 'They won't eat. They want to have their own sweeper – a black sweeper – and they won't take their meals until it is served to them by a Koori.'

'Well,' the boss said, frowning, 'what do you think?'

The veteran guard, put on the spot, replied, 'Let's give them their own wing. It will solve the problem we have right now and – who knows? – it might solve a few more.'

The boss nodded. *That just might work.*

*

Camberwell said he made the suggestion that would eventually become a policy: 'I suggested we could move all remand prisoners [those awaiting trial] into C Wing and put the Aboriginal blokes in D Wing. That way they would have their own wing and the problem would be solved. At that time the remand was in D Wing because it backed onto the Reception Centre [a prison wing that houses fresh inmates before they are moved to a permanent cell], but there was no reason it could not be moved.

'So they took the Aboriginal prisoners all out and put them in D Wing. It was ultimately the superintendent's decision, and we just thought it would be easy to swap them over to stop them from starving.

'After that we just turned around and said, "Here is your own wing. You can do whatever you want now. Sort out your issues amongst yourselves here."'

Soon Goulburn became less violent, the killings stopped and the number of bashings, standovers and stabbings dramatically dropped.

'It wasn't what we intended,' said Camberwell. 'But, yeah, the violence decreased. It was because the Aboriginal blokes were always causing a lot of trouble in the main jail, standing over other inmates. They were always a cause of the violence. They would stand over guys just for the sake of it. It could have been for shoes or something even more stupid. They were the guys that always had nothing, so they would take whatever they wanted. They would take whatever they could get.'

Camberwell said the Aboriginal inmates, however, would not stand over each other: 'None of them had anything worth taking. It solved a lot of problems.'

However, soon there were demands from others – first the Anglos and then the Islanders. Then the Middle Eastern inmates followed suit, and eventually the Chinese.

'Why are they so special?' inmates would ask. 'Why do they get their own wing? Give us the same.'

'They would threaten similar strikes, threaten to go off,' Camberwell said. 'What we had done so far was working, so we started the process of segregating the rest of them into different yards.'

A current guard explained how the inmates are split: 'There are four big wings in the prison,' he said. 'A, B, C and D. The two big wings are C and D, and they are divided up into four yards with roughly 30 inmates in each. One of those yards is called the Koori Yard, and that is where the Aboriginal inmates are kept. The others are called the Lebanese Yard, the Islander Yard and the Asian Yard. The Anglos can be placed in any of the yards. The yards all face onto each other and are separated by fences and razor wire.'

Racist?

Thus, in 1998, Goulburn unofficially became the only jail in Australia to racially segregate inmates. However, Kevin Camberwell is adamant the practice was never meant to be a policy: 'It was just a quick fix to stop the Aboriginal fellas from starving.'

The controversial move would be credited with ending the murderous Killing Fields period. It would also be condemned for sparking Goulburn's worst ever riot.

The practice was not made an official policy until 2002 when the Department of Corrective Services publicly revealed that the different ethnic groups were being isolated into separate yards.

A department spokesman said the policy, called 'ethnic clustering', had been introduced as a strategic move adopted to prevent violence and make difficult inmates more easily managed.

On 24 February 2005, just over two years after the Department of Corrective Services admitted to the policy of racial clustering in Goulburn, the US Supreme Court weighed in on the matter of racial segregation in prisons in both Texas and California, slamming the policy as both racist and of limited benefit.

In California, inmates were being assigned to a cell with a fellow inmate of the same race. The segregation was temporary, up to 60 days, and only put in place when necessary because a prisoner was a gang member or otherwise antagonistic towards to members of another race.

'We rejected the notion that separate can ever be equal 50 years ago in *Brown v. Board of Education*, and we refuse to resurrect it today,' Justice Sandra Day O'Connor said. 'When government officers are permitted to use race as a proxy for gang membership and violence without demonstrating a compelling government interest and proving that their means are narrowly tailored, society as a whole suffers.'

When the case was launched, US Solicitor General Paul Clement said the government could not separate people based on skin colour without the strongest of reasons.

Both he and the Supreme Court made repeated reference to the landmark American racism case of *Brown v. Board of Education* that held that racial segregation in 'separate but equal' schools was unconstitutional, including a 1968 decision barring blanket segregation in prisons.

So racial segregation in prisons – the same controversial practice still in place in Goulburn Jail in 2015 – was ordered to be abolished in Texas and in California in 2005.

Kevin Camberwell shrugs his shoulders and simply says the system works. 'It's good for that jail. For whatever reason, they just can't mix together at Goulburn because they'll end up fighting. It's hard to explain because you will send the same prisoners that are fighting [in Goulburn Jail] to Lithgow Jail, and they will mix with everyone.

'Goulburn has its own culture. They were climbing over each other for control. The different races . . . It was always a problem. They mixed with their own people better than anyone else, and that became a solution.

'It was just a case of them getting along better that way. They were a lot happier, and a lot happier to deal with. It's hard to say why it works – it just does.'

Former second-in-charge of New South Wales prisons Dave Farrell agrees: 'It certainly brought the harm down. But if you're a young Aboriginal and you were chucked in against ten or fifteen whitefellas, how would you feel? Some of them couldn't even speak English. They had certain benefits. I couldn't see any dramas with that. I know some people were offended by it, but we were keeping them, hopefully, within a harmonious environment.

'If you ask yourself the question, *If I was a young Aboriginal guy, who would I want to be with?* you would have to answer that you would want to be with your own. You're always going to have power struggles in jail, but they are more manageable this way.'

Most people who have worked at Goulburn Jail agree that the system of racial segregation works. Who would argue differently after the policy put an end to the Killing Fields?

Former Goulburn governor Allan Chisholm would, and he did – in the strongest possible way.

'That was one of my big issues,' Chisholm said. 'New South Wales prisons actually practised apartheid. That really gave me the shits. It was apartheid, pure and simple. That is all it can be when you separate all the inmates by race.

'It was already implemented before I got there, and there was nothing I could do to change it. It was, among other things, a union issue. It should have been stopped back then, and it certainly still shouldn't be going in this day and age.'

Former head of the New South Wales Department of Corrective Services Tony Vinson AM, the academic hired to implement the recommendations put forward by the Nagle Royal Commission into New South Wales Prisons in 1978, was also critical of the policy.

'There have always been segregation units,' Vinson, now a renowned social scientist and lecturer at the University of Sydney, said. 'Someone would be put in segregation for bad manners, or whatever. A Supreme Court judge declared that segregation as a means of extra punishment was inconsistent with the act. I did introduce the requirement that every prisoner put into segregation would be given a document to describe the reason for segregation. This would mean the prisoner would have something he could use to get legal assistance if it was wrongful segregation.

'Segregation is an issue, but when it comes to racial segregation, well, when I heard about this years later, I thought it was a terrible mistake. I knew it would increase violence.

'I have been in the best of jails, and one of the hallmarks of them is respect between the prisoners. You need to have an incubator of tolerance. I don't think people on the outside give a bugger about what's happening inside. We *should* be doing something about it because it's institutional racism. Among the people in the community who care, who would raise a concern . . . well, they probably have higher priorities. As far as elected politicians are concerned, the last thing they want to be accused of is any kind of softening of conditions in prisons, or any sympathy for particular groups.

'For example, the issue of the high proportion of Aboriginal prisoners, which is horrible, only gets crocodile tears annually. Racial segregation is a dreadful policy, and that's about all I can say about it.'

In 2002, the *Sydney Morning Herald* obtained an internal Corrective Services report that warned the practice of racial segregation 'only increases group tension' and is 'in nobody's best interest'. Prepared by a departmental policy advisor, the report slammed the jail's management policies as 'schizophrenic' and compared the prison to something out of George Orwell's novel *1984*.

'Some staff in key positions reflect a siege mentality and are totally convinced that any attempt to manage inmates other than in ethnically clustered groups will end in bloodshed,' the report said. 'Unless there is a commitment to meaningful change at Goulburn, it will remain the jail of last resort.'

A spokesman for the prisoners' advocacy group Justice Action told the *Herald* that the jail was run by a 'divide and conquer' technique designed to let prisoners live in fear of each other. This, the spokesman claimed, increased the power of prison officers and directed the antagonism of inmates against each other, rather than the guards.

A disturbance in March 2000, resulting in charges against 30 Aboriginal men, was also blamed on the policy. The Goulburn Local Court heard that frustrations over racial segregation and hatred, which had been building for months, had led Aboriginal prisoners to trash their cells.

'Some feel as though they are treated like animals,' said one of the inmate's representatives. 'The regime they live under is difficult to tolerate and [they] have responded in a destructive fashion. It has become a system of retribution and vengeance, rather than rehabilitation. They suffer daily, intolerable psychological abuse.'

And soon they would hit out. Oh, would they ever . . .

4

RIOTS

Remembering

Tim Swain shuts his eyes and shakes his fist. 'Come on, brain,' he stutters.

His head follows his hand: rocking *back* and then *forward*, *back* and then *forward*. A twitching nod at first, the movement becomes faster, angrier: *back, forward, back, forward.* Then harder, more violent: *back, forward, back, forward.*

Brain smacking into skull: *back, forward, back, forward.* He can't shake himself to sense.

'Nothing,' he says. 'Gone.'

Now his head is sadly still. He looks across the dining table, over the coffee he proudly made minutes before. Both the jubilation he found in being able to make a Nescafé – a spoon-and-sugar act he has only just reintroduced to his morning show – and the neck-flinging frustration of not being able to find a word are gone.

'Far-out,' he says, defeated. 'That day . . . It's hard.'

Small and slight of frame, he struggles not just to speak over sips of coffee about the day that ruined his life, but just to *speak*. Swain is a whisper of the man he was when he walked into Goulburn Correctional Centre on 16 April 2002 to begin, of all things, an overtime shift.

'I might not look it,' Swain says, 'but I was a very fit man. I loved – *loooved* – bikes. I raced them. I did . . . you know . . . come on, brain . . . the . . . the . . . wait, got it: the Canberra to Goulburn.'

Swain fumbles through a pile of newspaper clippings he has pulled from a folder once manila, now aged brown. He smiles and then points.

'See,' he beams, 'that's me.'

Lycra strangling his muscles, he is back-page news. 'Swain Wins Again' screams the headline, the local paper covering yet another of his two-wheeled triumphs.

'I just loved it,' he continues. 'Wish I could still love it now.'

His frantic fingers have filled the dining table, sun-soaked at the back of his lonesome one-bedroom battleaxe, with newspaper cut-outs. He is suddenly distracted.

'That's him,' Swain says, pointing at another newspaper. 'You know? It's . . . him. Him that did this, you know?'

Swain is pointing at a photo of the man who put him in hospital for 11 months, including five weeks in a coma. His finger shakes as it hovers over the image of the criminal. This is no longer a back-page sports story in the local paper. It's the front page of Sydney's Sunday *Herald*.

The headline: 'Australia's Most Violent Prisoners'.

Swain stares down at the man who cost him his job, his house, his wife.

'Oh well,' he says. 'That's the price I paid. It wasn't his fault. It was the job. I knew that it could happen, and so does everyone else who works there. That's Goulburn.'

Swain takes eight pills a day and has been diagnosed with post-traumatic epilepsy.

He still can't read or write. Mail is stacked in his kitchen, little envelopes wrapped in rubber bands. *Bills? Insurance pay-outs? Mortgage statements?* He doesn't know, and he won't know until he can find someone who will come over and read them to him. There were plenty of volunteers at first – he was front-page news, after all – but now the news-print is yellow and torn at the edges, and Tim is running out of rubber bands.

Swain's ex-wife, Jane, sits beside him for his first-ever interview. She helps him with his words when he is stuck, and recalls the things he can't remember.

'We were booked to go on a holiday just 23 days later,' says Jane. 'We were going on a six-week trip of a lifetime. We'd been saving up for it since before we got married. The night it happened . . . I remember sitting there and thinking about the trip. I was told he had a fractured skull, and I was just like, *Okay, fractured skull – he should be okay for the trip.* I had no idea. I had to cancel it two days later, and then I was sitting in the hospital with Tim's dad getting "that chat",

69

the one you see in movies. It was about the life support, and whether or not to turn it off. The doctor said I might want to think about it, and we did because we knew Tim wouldn't want to live his life as a vegetable.'

The machine kept him going, the plug was never pulled.

'It ruined my life,' Swain says. 'Everything was taken away from me. I just wanted someone to kill me. I wanted to be dead.'

Swain is finally ready to confront his demons. He has agreed to talk about the day his skull was shattered and a piece of his brain was left on the prison floor.

Didgeridoos and Table Legs

Swain looked at his fellow guard.

'Stop bitching, mate,' he said. 'It's not that bad. It's a job and it pays the bills. Quit if you don't like it.'

Swain had had enough of the complaining guard – a young rookie fresh to the job.

Oh well, Swain thought. *It's only for one shift.*

Swain was counting the days down to his belated honeymoon; 23 sleeps until he would be in Canada with the love of his life and fellow Goulburn employee, Jane. He had taken today's shift in B Wing as a one-off. The usual guards were sick, maybe some were on holidays.

Think of the money.

He climbed high above the landing and into the metal warders' cage.

'Mate, zip it and do your job,' Swain said. 'They will be coming up soon. Keep your eyes open.'

Swain and the young officer perched over the prison on west watch, waiting for the inmates to return to their cells. Swain looked across the wing – all concrete, steel and violent men. His back-up, Robert Hursey, a veteran guard nearing retirement, and Sharon Madden, a young woman just starting her career, were in another metal cage.

East watch is in position.

Swain looked down at his watch: 2.59pm. The inmates, 30 in this maximum-security wing today, had a minute to muster. The murderers, rapists and thieves would have their names marked off a list before returning to their cells with their evening meals. Or so Swain and his fellow officers thought.

'What the fuck is he doing,' inquired junior, pointing towards a hefty inmate dragging a table along the cold concrete floor.

'Shit,' Swain muttered.

And then the madness began. In four minutes, Swain's dreams – and his body – would be crushed.

The prisoner hoisted the table over his head before hurling it to the ground.

Crash!

The table exploded.

'Get 'em!' screamed a wiry inmate as he scooped up a dislodged table leg: 15 centimetres by 15 centimetres of Australian hardwood. 'Come on!'

A posse of frenzied inmates kicked and grabbed at the wreckage, turning the splinters into weapons. Others darted into cells, reappearing with more broken furniture, metal shivs – even a didgeridoo. Swain looked at the cage door; it was locked. He and junior were safe. They would wait for the reinforcements to rush in with their shields, batons and, most importantly, their tear gas.

'Oh no,' Swain said, looking west. The rabid mob, fully armed and rampant, was rushing towards the other end of the wing.

'Kill the dogs!' the prisoners cried as they stormed towards Bob and Sharon.

Something was wrong.

'Their latch is open,' Swain yelled. 'They're not locked in.'

Bob was not getting any younger, but Swain knew the war veteran could handle himself. But a woman? Swain cringed.

'She is going to get raped,' Tim said. 'We have to help.'

Swain unlocked the latch and pushed open the cage door – the only thing keeping him safe from the 30 maximum-security inmates, now armed and threatening to kill. The metal slapped shut as he and the rookie officer began their charge, junior ready to put his life on the line for a couple of strangers and a job he didn't want.

The noise was deafening. The inmates were screaming and shouting, bashing and banging.

Swain and junior were sprinting halfway up the wing, rushing across the landing towards the prisoners and their prey, when . . .

Whack!

Swain saw the blow coming, a flash of wood rushing towards his skull. But there was nothing he could do – no time to duck, dodge or dive. An inmate, one that had it in for Swain, had launched from a cell and driven a table leg into the side of his head. The wood cracked Swain's skull, the force of the blow lifting him off his feet. The officer was down but not out. Blood rushed from a gaping wound in his head; he dragged himself from the floor.

Crash! Smack! Bang!

The inmates came in from everywhere. Kicking. Punching. Swinging. Stomping. The pain was excruciating. And then everything went black.

'The code red was called and we all just stopped,' recalls Jane, who was working in the Emergency Response Unit on the day of the attack. 'We could tell by the voices on the radio that it wasn't your usual disturbance, that it wasn't a prison yard fight or even a brawl. And I knew it was Tim that was in trouble, even then, because I knew he was working in there at the time. There were only four officers in there, and I knew he would have been in the thick of it.'

Jane 'geared-up', a term officers use for putting on protective clothing and arming themselves with batons and tear gas, and bolted to B Wing.

'It was over in four minutes,' Jane says. 'We raced over but a response team was already deploying gas. There was gas everywhere, and they were dragging them out, one by one.'

Jane looked across at the man lying on the stretcher. The officer's blue prison shirt was now red. He was not moving.

'I didn't even know it was Tim,' Jane says. 'They were all going to be injured, so I guess I didn't think too much about it.'

The man covered in blood was indeed her husband. A nurse was pushing against his broken skull to keep his brains in.

'The nurse was with him, so I thought, *That's good,*' Jane continues. 'So I just ran into the wing to do my job. I helped put the last few inmates away and came out, not thinking about it at all.'

The riot now over, a fellow officer confronted Jane: 'You better come with me. You need to be with Tim.'

Jane was led towards an ambulance.

'I had no idea if it was serious,' Jane says. 'I just thought, *There he is and he is being treated.* They told me to go to hospital with him. There were at least ten who needed to be taken to hospital that day, and Tim was just one of them.'

Or so Jane thought.

There were signs – not in blazing neon, but more the invisible-ink variety.

'It was the Aboriginal wing,' said former 2IC of B Wing Ian Norris. 'At the time, they were segregating inmates by race because of all the racial problems. We had known tensions were high. Myself and the senior, John Walker, had talked about it. We even reported that something could happen. It's the type of thing you get a feel for, not something visible. Not something you have proof of. You get a feel for the way the inmates are reacting and talking to you. It's almost like they are talking to you but they are not really switched on to what they are saying. They had a way of sort of fobbing you off. I can't say that they did this or did that; it was just a general mood. They were being really polite before the attack, and that tells you to watch your back. We did searches through the wings – we do six random ones every day – and we found little notes and things and gave them to the intel officers. They said it was nothing. John and I had worked in the wing for a few weeks on a permanent basis, and we were picking up things from the scumbags.'

The inmates, at least the timid ones, were asking to be locked away.

'That's a pretty good sign that something is going on,' Norris said. 'They want to keep away from trouble. Inmates were scared and wanted to be on their own. We told the governor that something was going on, but we weren't sure what. You need to tell them if you get that feeling because you cover your arse if the shit hits the fan.'

The warning was dismissed.

'The governor didn't feel like it was necessary to take any action. If they were certain something was going to happen, they would lock down the wing. They would do a full ramp through the wing for hidden weapons and things like that. But he let this one slide. He didn't think there was anything going on, just a little bit of tension between the inmates. We thought he was probably right.'

He wasn't.

'Ronald Priestly was just a nasty piece of work,' said Norris of the man who had already put the hit on Colombian drug dealer Lara-Gomez. 'He had an evil tongue. He was always ranting and raving, carrying on like an idiot.'

Ronald Priestly, from Moree, New South Wales, was serving a sentence of 32 years for murder. He was a career criminal, first jailed when he was ten. He was known as 'Big Daddy', and with attack dog James Sonny Paulson by his side, he ruled the wing.

'They weren't the sort of blokes you'd mess about with,' Norris said. 'If there was something going on, they were involved. Because of [Priestly's] manner, you couldn't really put anything he'd say aside. You would always have to take it seriously and put it in your case notes. The other crims seemed to listen to him, and I don't know for the life of me why. He was always in the shit for something. He had certainly spent time in the High-Security Unit for trying to thump an officer. They put him in there for a couple of weeks to calm down, and when he came back he was fine.'

But not for long.

'He started getting angry,' Norris continued. 'Like any crim, it doesn't take long for them to get pissed off about something else. There was talk he was pissed off because an officer said something to him in a yard. Maybe someone threatened him or told him he was nothing. We thought, *What sort of idiot would say that?* I have no idea whether that's true or not, but that's what was going around.'

Priestly's anger was contagious.

'It was one of those small wings and it didn't take much to fire them up,' Norris said. 'It had about 35 or 40 cells on top, and it was mostly two-out. There was one four-out cell. The maximum capacity of the wing would have been 50 or so [inmates], but there were only 30 in it at the time.'

'I actually enjoyed working in that wing,' Norris continued. 'It was reasonably quiet and I had experience with Aboriginal people. But it was a pretty miserable place to look at with nothing but concrete walls and a steel table.'

Priestly and Paulson instigated the riot. They had stockpiled weapons and stirred discontent.

'I was on two days off when it happened,' Norris said. 'I don't know who threw the first punch, but I know they were both involved. The crims were very well prepared. They had table legs broken off, ready for action, wet towels ready to be used as gas masks. There is no doubt Priestly started it. He was the type of bloke who made the bullets and gave them to someone else to fire.'

Jane agrees: 'They were the ringleaders alright. They had weapons ready and had planned the whole thing. We think they were actually planning it for later in the week. The riot happened on Tuesday, but things that have come out later say it was planned for the Thursday. Priestly had been locked up in the pound for three days and came out very angry. He said, "Stuff it – let's do this thing today."

'There wasn't a regular staff member in that wing on that day. All the officers were doing overtime. Their timing was perfect. Priestly should not have even been in that wing. He should have been in segregation. He had behavioural issues and had been sanctioned. But they let him out. Even the way they did the muster wasn't right. Unit 4 should have been last, which would have allowed more staff to be there, but it wasn't. It was the most dangerous wing and, for some reason, they mustered Yard 4 first. If only a couple of things were different, it may not have happened.'

But happen it did – and it was Goulburn's worst ever riot. Ten officers were injured in less than four minutes, and the 30 prisoners caused a staggering $1.8 million worth of damage.

'You should have seen all the shit,' Norris said. 'And I am talking shit, literally. Shit had gone all over the floor when they had smashed their toilets, and they were also using shit as a weapon, throwing it around. I was one of the guys who went in wearing a bio-suit after the police had finished their forensic investigation, and I spent a week cleaning shit from walls. We hired high-pressure water jets. It was a horrible job . . . The stench was just unbearable. And blood was everywhere – on the walls, the floor. It really was a sickening sight.'

The inmates had trashed everything in the wing.

'The beds were destroyed,' Norris said. 'They'd been concreted into the wall with massive stirrup bolts, but that didn't stop them from ripping them off. They tore toilets off, too . . . and shelves, cabinets and tables, which they used as blockades to try and stop the emergency units from getting in. They dislodged everything with their bare hands or smashed them to bits with table legs. I was shocked to see the damage; the water damage alone was huge. Police had been in there for a week doing forensic work before we were allowed to clean it up. It was hot, hard, heavy work. A week or two later the contractors started putting it back together. All the bedding had to be replaced; it all had to be retiled. The whole wing had to be refurnished. Everything was broken.'

And so was Tim Swain, now in hospital in an induced coma.

Changing Channels

Jane walked into the stark-white room and looked down at her husband.

'There was a post-it note stuck on the side of his head,' she recalls. 'It said "don't touch".'

A machine was the only thing keeping Swain alive: *blip . . . blip . . . blip.* Half his skull was now missing, all soft tissue and exposed brain.

'Tim was airlifted to Canberra,' Jane continues. 'He needed emergency surgery because his skull was fractured and his brain was swelling up. He went in for the surgery at 1am and then was placed in an induced coma.'

Doctors feared Swain would never wake up. They were sure he had suffered brain damage, but to what extent they didn't know. *Blip . . . blip . . . blip.*

Jane and Tim Swain's father considered pulling the plug.

'I don't know why we didn't,' Jane says. 'There were just little signs that gave us hope.'

Swain opened his eyes five weeks later.

'The swelling in his brain had gone down, and they were able to turn off the machine. We didn't think he would make it, but he was so fit and healthy. I'm sure any other officer would not have survived. He didn't drink or smoke, and he was athletic. His strength got him through. Well, it kept him alive anyway.'

Tubes flew, ripping from his arm as he slammed the hospital bed.

Pherrrrrrr. Drool poured from the edges of Swain's mouth as he shouted babble. He hit the bed again, crying more incoherencies. *Bbuuuu-balaaaaa.* 'I couldn't even talk for two years,' Swain says. 'I think that was probably the worst part, because it was a living nightmare. I could still think fine, and I knew what I wanted to say. I just couldn't get the words out. I would end up screaming. I couldn't tell people what I wanted. I remember wanting coffee, little things like that, and I had no way to tell anyone. I was telling them in my mind, but my mouth was saying nothing.'

Jane, utterly helpless, endured the painful tantrums.

'He would end up beating himself and the bed,' she says. 'He was trying to tell us something, and we were looking around, trying to work it out – things like having the channel changed – and he would end up losing it. It was horrible.'

Swain, a skeletal 38kg after emerging from the coma, knew people were laughing at him.

'There were [hospital staff and friends] that thought I was retarded and treated me like it,' Swain says.

'They were smartarses, and I couldn't do anything about them. Some people thought it was funny. That really pissed me off.'

Swain was alive, but sometimes he did not want to be.

'I was useless. At times I just wanted someone to kill me. My memory is still bad, and I remember weird things about that time. I can't remember coming out of the coma, and I only remember thinking that I had no memory for about two or three weeks, but really six months had been wiped out.'

Swain can now talk. He stumbles and stutters, but he can talk. He can also walk, cook and shop for himself.

'I even built that kitchen,' he says, pointing to a shiny new cooktop.

But Swain will never be the man he was.

'They cut a big piece of my brain out and I will never get it back,' he says. 'I am missing the front part that affects speech and some of my movement. I can't say lots of words, and it took me a year to learn how to walk. Damn, that was hard.'

Prison Payback

SPLASH!

The water slapped against their cold, naked bodies, the ten rioters shivering as they huddled together in a hopeless bid to keep warm.

'Give us some fucking clothes, you dogs!' one of them screamed. 'You can't do this!'

Wayne Connors, Colin Davis, Craig Lardner, Aaron Maher, Joshua Mansfield, James Paulson, Ronald Priestly, Dwayne Welsh, John Weston and Daniel Barker were all identified as major players in the April 2002 riot. They were the men who stomped, smashed and slapped the officers. They were the inmates who swung sticks and drove didgeridoos. They were the attackers who injured seven guards and put Swain in a coma.

And now several Corrective Services officers began dishing out jailhouse justice.

In a gross violation of their human rights, the inmates were stripped naked and doused with buckets of ice-cold water as payback for the riot. They were also assaulted.

Slap.

A booming overhead; an open-handed right thudded into an inmate's ear. He fell to the ground, writhing in agony.

Bang.

Another guard, another prisoner, same result: inmate on the ground, a blubbering mess.

Twelve years after the riot, a former officer involved in the 'clean-up', speaking on the condition of anonymity, has now revealed what they were ordered to do to the prisoners after they were herded into a holding cell in the aftermath.

'They were made to feel very uncomfortable and doused with buckets of water every now and then,' said the officer. 'We made sure they had that cold feeling and were treated in a way that got some payback. It was payback, plain and simple. They threatened to turn it on if we didn't give them clothes and whatever else. They carried on a bit, but we were all geared up and ready to go.'

The officer said he and the team of wardens who were sent to watch the inmates and respond to any further violent behavior were told to breach department policy.

'We were told not to use any video cameras under any circumstance,' said the officer. 'Whatever action that took place would not be recorded. Whenever we stepped into the cells, there was no record of it. That is totally against departmental procedure, but that was the order.'

The officer also claimed the inmates were physically assaulted after making threatening comments while locked in the cell.

'They were left naked and wet until the next day,' the former officer continued. 'They went at us and started jumping up and down. They started yelling. Some of these guys knew us by name, and they'd seen us around and knew what we were like. They yelled at us and wouldn't stop. One of the officers took some serious offence to what was said, and he looked over at us – it was one in, all in. We went down to the cell, opened it up and he gave one of them an overhand slap to the ear. It knocked him pretty much into next year. Another officer got off a shot and the guy dropped straight to the ground. Some of the others came in and gave them a few clips around the ear. It was a case of, *If you want to play the game then we will too.*

'They all started crying and huddled back up. Even though they were nude, they were all huddled into a group. Paulson and Priestly were crybabies – they were the ones that cried the most. We had broken them by 2am and they were nothing but blubbering babies.'

The ten men, who all stood trial for the riot with charges ranging from affray to attempted murder, alleged they had been mistreated.

'They complained about it to their legal representative,' said the officer. 'I think it was the legal rep that brought it up in court. I was under the impression that if they even mentioned it again or told their legal reps the story again, their lives would not be worth living in jail.'

Gone Girls

I push Tim Swain on what he can remember about Priestly and Paulson, about broken table legs and didgeridoos.

'I can remember that,' Swain says. He stops talking and shakes his head. And then he cries. 'But it's what I *can't* remember that hurts. There is a huge chunk before the attack that is missing, and that hurts more than remembering the attack. The worst is my kids – I can't remember anything of my daughters. Their whole childhood has just been wiped out. They were young when it happened, about 11 or 12, and I can't remember anything about them. It's gone. It's all gone . . .'

Swain composes himself.

'Sorry, but that really pisses me off,' he continues. 'It makes me angry.'

Swain then turns his mind back to 16 April 2002.

'There were six or seven blokes in the wing that were especially bad. They didn't like me and they wanted me dead. I think it was a plan to kill me. I'm sure they were after me. They planned to get me. I had problems with them for years, and now they were after me.'

Swain then breaks out in a smile. He is reflecting on one of his few good memories.

'I'm thinking about when I saw them in court,' he says enthusiastically. 'You know, the buggers who did this. They all pleaded not guilty because they thought I couldn't give evidence, that I couldn't talk. I practised for hours, and when I got up I managed to say my name. When I walked out past the box, I hit the glass, pointed at them and, you know.' He sticks his finger up. 'After that they all pleaded guilty. That felt pretty good.'

Lessons Learned – Rioting in 2014

In September 2014, an incident declared in headlines as the 'Worst Riot At Goulburn In More Than A Decade' was downplayed by the Department of Corrective Services as a minor disturbance. The stand-off between guards and Yard 6 also caused a stink between the *Daily Telegraph* and the ABC – the former, who broke the story, claiming religion was a factor, the latter saying it was not. Decide for yourself.

'Hey,' shouted the inmate to a female guard. 'Yeah you, you fucking cunt. I'll chop your head off and post it on the internet. You're a fucking DOG.'

The guard was furious and reported the comments to her superior.

'That's disgusting behaviour,' said the boss, 'and I'm sick of this kind of shit. Lay misconduct charges on those involved and send the rest of them a message. Take away their bloody barbecue – it's a privilege, not a right.'

And so it began . . .

Yard 6, the Koori Yard, is located in C Wing. It holds an average of 30 prisoners at any particular time. The exclusive-to-Goulburn policy of racial segregation sees the Koori Yard nestled between the Islander Yard and the Muslim Yard. Racist? Absolutely. Disputed? Rarely. On 20 September 2014, there were 33 inmates in the yard.

And boy, were they pissed . . .

'The barbecue was an excuse,' said an officer involved in the riot. 'It gave them a reason to cause shit. The Koori Yard is constantly carrying on. They have an us-against-the-world mentality, and anything that happens to them happens to them because they are black. Officially the incident occurred because the barbecue was taken away, but it was just the spark they needed to set a fire.

'Things like barbecues are a control measure in jail. You give them good things like barbecues when they behave, and you take them away when they don't. Unfortunately, they can use something like this as an excuse for something bigger.'

'Fuck you, pricks,' screamed an inmate, directing his senseless slander through the knotted wire fence. 'You're a fucking dog. All of yous are fucking dog scum.'

Another joined in. 'Yeah, suck on this,' he said, pointing at his gyrating pelvis.

Another joined in. Three then four . . . and eventually all 35.

'There were half a dozen instigators,' said a guard, who requested anonymity. 'It started with just yelling, a lot of carrying on. It was the usual shit.'

But it kept on going, growing louder, more frequent, more potent.

'They kept at it,' the officer said, 'and I think it was thanks to a couple of individuals in particular. Two known agitators were in the yard at the time – Damien [Glenn] Featherstone and Conrad Craig. They had been in and out of Goulburn for the last six years. They are both Muslims who converted to Islam while in jail, and they are both shitbags with big mouths. They are young and angry, but others listen to them.'

Clunk.

A tin can landed next to an officer's foot. The inmate had filled it with urine before throwing it over the barb-wire-topped cyclone fence. Predictably, and uselessly, most of the piss ended up back on him, the rest splashing on the concrete ground and metal fence.

'That's when it became more than words,' said the officer. 'First a tin full of piss and then whatever else they had – milk cartons, food, even shoes. We hadn't formed into squads yet; we were just monitoring and hoping that it would not escalate.'

More tins filled with piss and flying shoes sufficed as 'escalation'.

'It was then that the emergency squads started gearing up. They slapped on armour, grabbed shields and loaded the gas . . .'

An officer demanded to know what they wanted. He was met with silence . . . and a carton of piss.

'The officers on the ground tried talking to them,' continued the officer. 'But the crims did not want a bar of it. They refused to talk to anyone other than the prison deputy. They were refusing to muster – they muster at 2.30 every afternoon – and by 2.10 we knew that they were not going to muster for sure. Management came down and tried to talk to them.'

The inmates refused, while reloading cartons and tins.

'Get the boss,' they screamed. 'Get the boss, you fucking DOGS.'

The call was made to the boss, considering the reason behind the riot was the barbecue.

'He came in in a pair of thongs and a T-shirt,' said the officer. 'He was on a day off, but I guess that's why they pay him the big bucks. It also proves that this wasn't something minor, as was suggested by some.'

The boss asked them what was going on, what was wrong and what could he do to make them stop throwing shit and return to their cells.

'It was a tricky situation,' said the highly experienced guard, 'because you can't give them what they want. You can't capitulate. If you give in to them, you are reinforcing bad behaviour.'

The manager of security told the inmates that, because of their disgraceful comments to the female guard that morning, they wouldn't be getting the barbecue back. It's a privilege, not a right . . .

By now the officers had formed into squads. They were all geared up, gassed up and itching to go.

Exterior view of Goulburn Jail. (JOHN GRAINGER/NEWSPIX)

Correctional officers at the gates to Unit 7 of the High-Risk Management Unit, known as Supermax. (BRAD HUNTER/NEWSPIX)

All along the watchtower. The forbidding walls and guard towers overlooking Goulburn Jail – Australia's most secure prison. (TOP: SANDRA PRIESTLEY/NEWSPIX, BOTTOM: ADAM TAYLOR/NEWSPIX)

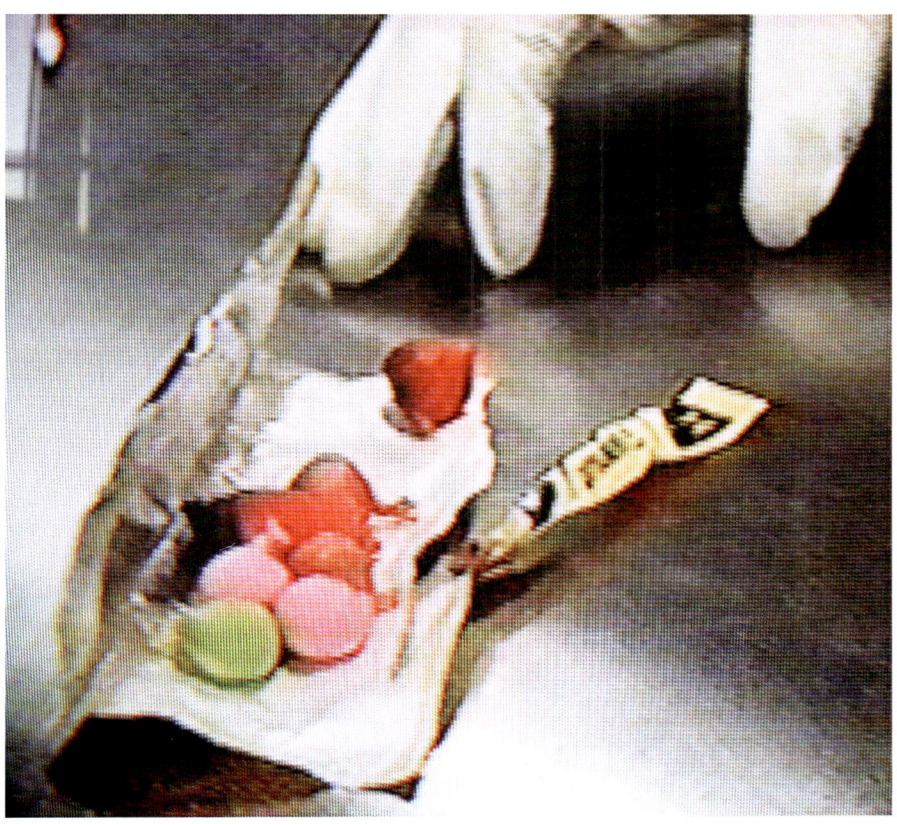

Cannabis weighing 11 grams wrapped in balloons and two mobile phone SIM cards found in an M&M wrapper brought in by a visitor during a security lockdown. (SARAH RHODES/NEWSPIX)

Crystal methamphetamine – 'ice' – has become an epidemic in Goulburn Jail. 'Ice can give some men the strength of 20 bulls,' one officer said. (CRAIG GREENHILL/NEWSPIX)

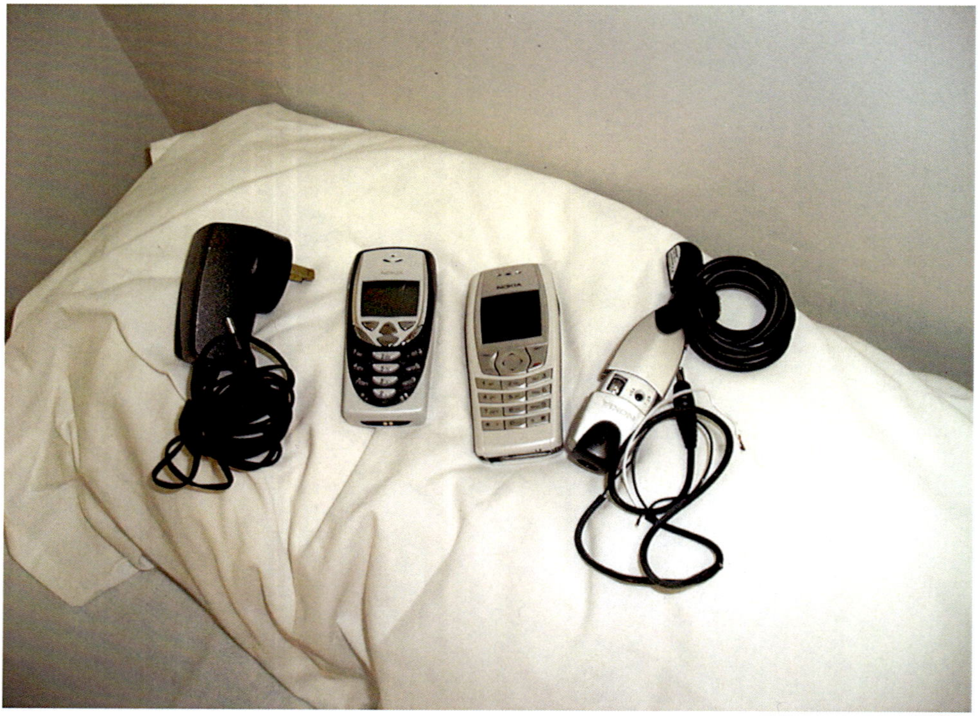

Contraband mobile phones and chargers seized from Supermax. (AAP IMAGE/DEPARTMENT OF CORRECTIVE SERVICES)

Former New South Wales Premier Bob Carr, along with Governor David White, at the opening of Supermax, 1 June 2011. (JOHN FEDER/NEWSPIX)

Supermax prison officers stand at attention. (JOHN FEDER/NEWSPIX)

An aerial shot of the Supermax complex. The main prison and sandstone entrance are to the upper left.

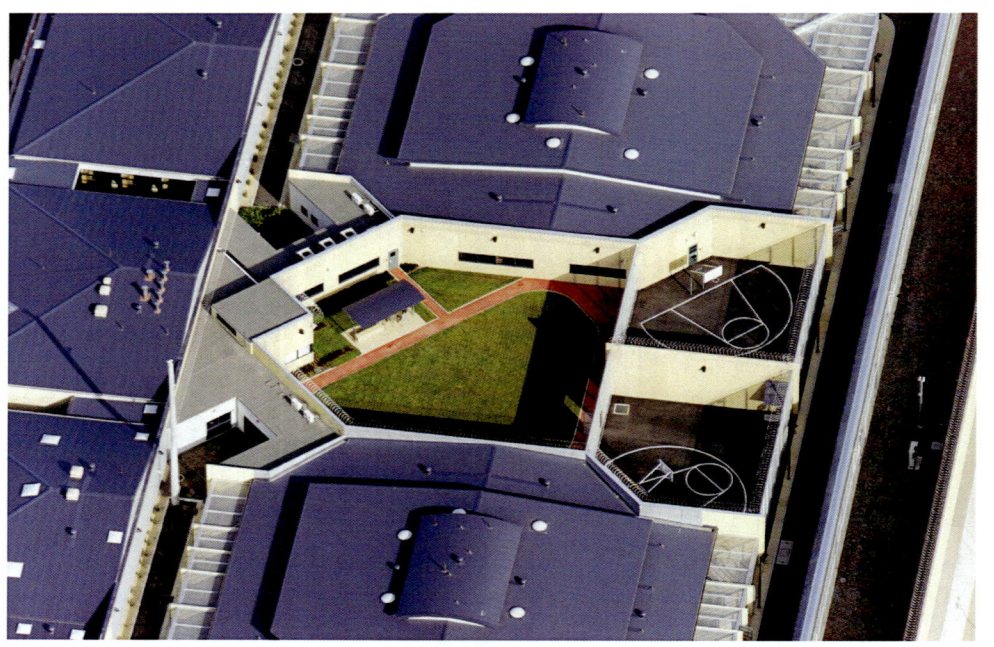

A close-up of the Supermax complex, detailing the basketball courts and red outdoor athletics track. Opposition MP Andrew Humpherson felt the facility more closely resembled a luxury hotel than a maximum-security prison for Australia's worst criminals.
(BOTH PHOTOS BY BARRY CHAPMAN/FAIRFAX PHOTOS)

'Abandon all hope, ye who enter here.' A correctional officer stands at the entrance to Supermax.

An officer jogs during his break on the athletics track in the Unit 7 yard of Supermax. Note the garden that serial killer Lindsay Rose was paid $12 a week to weed and water.
(BOTH PHOTOS BY BRAD HUNTER/NEWSPIX)

The clinical, well-lit hallways inside Supermax. What goes on behind those thick cell doors is the stuff of horror, shame and secrecy. (ADAM TAYLOR/NEWSPIX)

The inside of an isolated Supermax cell. The bed is a concrete slab fixed to the wall; a 25-centimetre-thick piece of foam serves as a mattress. (BRAD HUNTER/NEWSPIX)

A phone inside a cage where Supermax inmates can book in to make calls, pending approval from the commissioner's office.

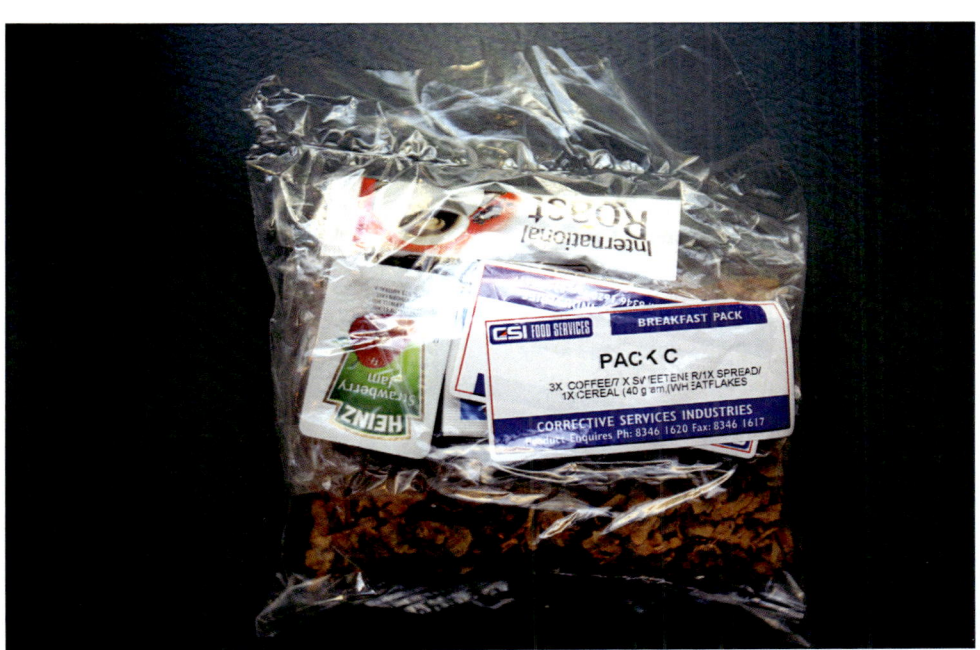

A breakfast pack for one of the Supermax inmates. The contents include coffee, sweetener, strawberry jam and cereal. (BOTH PHOTOS BY ADAM TAYLOR/NEWSPIX)

Star of the hit TV show *Hey Dad..!*, Robert Hughes had an epic fall from grace when he was convicted of ten sexual and indecent assault charges involving five girls between the ages of seven and 15 years old. (NEWS LTD/NEWSPIX)

Robert Hughes arrives at the Downing Centre Local Court in Sydney with his wife, Robyn Gardiner. Hughes received a prison sentence of up to ten years and nine months. In the sentencing, Judge Peter Zahra noted, 'The offender does not express remorse, and there is no evidence that the offender remained troubled by his conduct.' (ADAM TAYLOR/NEWSPIX)

Confessed murderer and kidnapper Robert Mark Steele, who was involved in a siege and subsequent shootout with police at Hanging Rock Station, Cangai, on 29 June 2001. According to former Goulburn Jail Governor Allan Chisholm, 'He was simple but kind, and could have destroyed anyone in the jail but didn't.'
(GREG NEWINGTON/NEWSPIX)

Lindsay Rose confessed to murdering five people and was sentenced to five consecutive life terms without the possibility of parole. He now spends his time tending to his chronic haemorrhoids and writing complaint letters concerning inmate conversions to Islam.
(NEWS LTD/NEWSPIX)

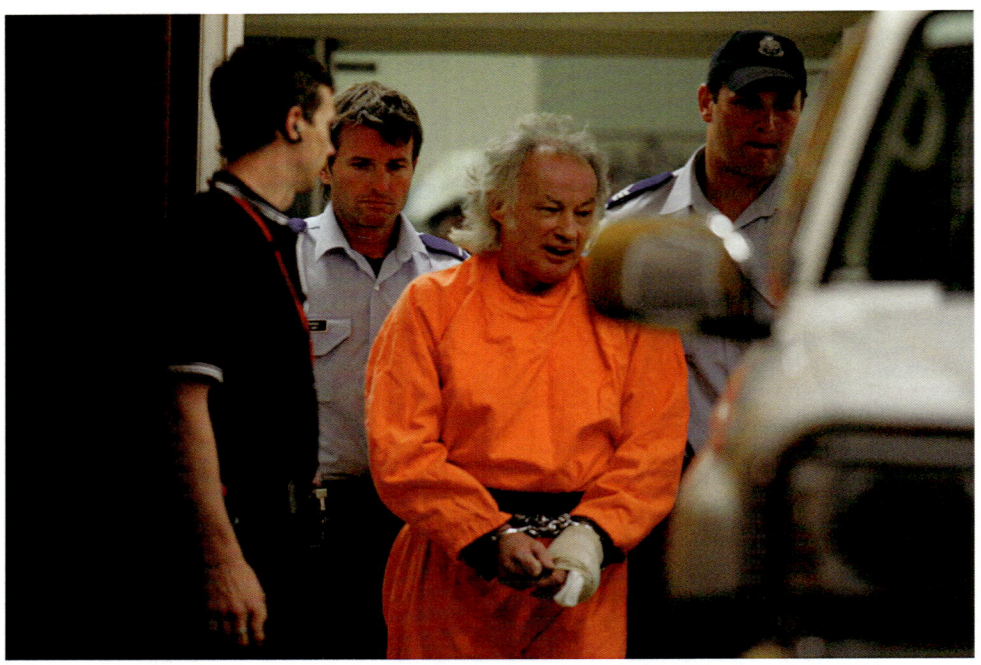

Notorious serial killer Ivan Milat being escorted out of Goulburn Hospital and back to prison after cutting off his own finger and attempting to post it to the High Court. (GARY RAMAGE/NEWSPIX)

Former Corrective Services Commissioner Dr Leo Keliher holds a hacksaw blade found in a packet of arrowroot biscuits in Ivan Milat's Supermax cell. (SANDRA PRIESTLEY/NEWSPIX)

Police officers take drug dealer and gang member Michael Kanaan away from his house in Belfield following a 32-hour siege. Kanaan is serving three life sentences plus 50 years and four months, without the possibility of parole, for murdering three people in 1998. (ADAM HOLLINGWORTH/NEWSPIX)

Brothers 4 Life gang founder Bassam Hamzy has been described as the most dangerous inmate in the correctional system.

Jihadist Faheem Lodhi, the first convicted Australian terrorist under new 2005 legislation.

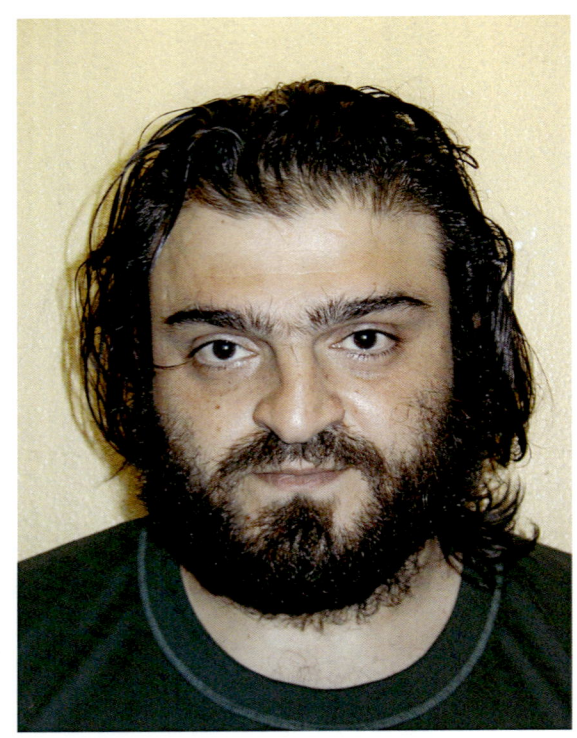

Moustafa Cheiko

Khaled Cheiko

Four of the 'Terror Five' militants arrested in 2005 and convicted of stockpiling high-powered guns and homemade bombs to inflict mass death and destruction in Sydney.

Mohamed Elomar

Abdul Hasan

Gang rapist Bilal Skaf leaving King Street Supreme Court. In his sentencing remarks, Judge Michael Finnane concluded, 'What this trial showed was that he was the leader of the pack, a liar, a bully, a coward, callous and mean – the worst of all offenders who conducted himself as if the proceedings were a joke.' (NICK MOIR/FAIRFAX PHOTOS)

'You just can't give them a win,' said the officer. 'No matter how small. You can't, because down the line someone will end up getting seriously hurt.'

The order was given: 'Shut it down.'

Clink . . . Clink . . . Clink.

Metal hit metal, the cell locks snapping shut as every inmate in the prison – except those ready to riot – were put away.

'All the other areas of the jail were shut,' the officer said. 'Supermax included. The officers from Supermax geared up and came down to help. We were lucky because at this stage it was contained. The spontaneous acts of violence that occur in riots often spread without warning. They can get out of hand very quickly. You need a response team in immediately, and the prison action plan has to be put into place.'

'Allahu akbar,' came the cry from the Muslim Yard as the now formed-up officers stood in front of wings A, B, C and D. 'Kill the DOGS!'

'We were left with the four yards in the main wing,' the officer recalled. 'The Muslim inmates were at the back, and they were egging the Aboriginals on. Then we had the Islanders next door, looking like they wanted to get involved too.'

First the Asian inmates mustered; they put their hands up and allowed the guards to lock them away in their cells. They were having no part of this. And then, despite the jihadist-shouting and tough-talking, the Muslims surrendered – not that they ever got started.

'They came to the front of the yard and saw 100 officers in full riot gear and shat their pants,' the officer continued. 'A lot of these Lebanese blokes are very brave when the odds are in their favour. But when they saw a couple of squads and knew we weren't going to muck around, they mustered like good little inmates.'

The fence shook as the Aboriginal inmate climbed.

Thud.

He hit the ground on the other side, then bolted across the small concrete section before scaling the next wire fence.

Thud.

He was now standing in another yard, facing 30 angry Islanders.

'Some of them ripped the razor wire,' the officer said. 'And one of them went over. The Islanders told him to piss off, but they armed him up before he went back. The Islanders then began throwing stuff over the fence to them, things they could use as projectiles or weapons.'

The final warning was delivered to the Islanders: *Go back to your cells or else.*

Four of the inmates took the threat seriously, one of them the notorious armed robber and hit-and-run murderer William Ngati.

'One of the guys that went back in was the guy that killed Skye [19-month-old Skye Sassine] during a police chase,' the officer said. 'He was responsible for creating "Skye's Law" [legislation that carries a maximum five-year jail sentence for failing to stop for police]. That was a bit of a shock because he was involved in a disturbance recently where he assaulted an officer with a tin of tuna. The other 26 refused to go back in.'

So the armed and armoured squads were left facing 56 rabid inmates.

'It escalated and got to the point where they were throwing more shit,' the officer said. 'Brevilles, toasters – whatever they could find. The instigators were on the roof of an old tin humpy. And, believe it or not, one bloke was running around with a plastic bag over his head. I guess it was a makeshift gas mask, but suffocating yourself probably isn't the best idea. We all thought that was pretty funny.'

The proclamation was delivered: 'I'm giving you a direction to move to the front of the yard and muster. If you fail to comply, force may be used.'

One of the inmates stopped rampaging to reply, 'Piss off,' before getting back to the ripping, tearing and throwing.

Pop. Pop.

Two 40-millimetre canisters were shot into the air. They whizzed over the fence.

Clink. Clink.

The canisters fell to the concrete, each spewing five pods of noxious, stinging, mucus-inducing gas.

And the inmates screamed. Oh boy, did they scream.

'The sounds they made were just horrible,' the Corrections officer continued. 'Painful. The pods burn a pyrotechnic tear gas, and it's real nasty stuff. It hits you anywhere you sweat – crotch, eyes, mouth, armpits – anywhere there's moisture. It stings and it burns. You can't see, you can't breathe, and mucus spews out of your mouth and nose. It feels like you're having an asthma attack.'

The prisoners screamed, they ran, and they dropped.

'But it was decided it wasn't having the desired effect because of the size of the yard,' the officer said. So out came the gas grenades and the 'foggers'. 'They sent in a couple of grenades to herd them towards the middle. The two instigators were still on the roof, jumping up and down, untouched by the gas, so another team went and started clearing them with foggers. The fogger is an aerosol canister. It is highly pressurised and it shoots chlorobenzalmalononitrile. It has a range of about 16 feet, and it is instantaneous.'

The Mortein for inmates worked.

'It's like watching bugs drop from the ceiling after hitting them with flyspray. They fell from the roof and into the front of the yard.'

Crack.

The lock was snapped and the cavalry charged.

'Anyone that was left standing was chopped down,' the officer continued. 'A couple of them decided to fight, but most didn't. A team went through the front. By then it was just a mass of guys screaming and crying like girls. They didn't want to be in there anymore.'

Some begged.

'Lock me up, boss,' they said. 'I want to muster. I'm not here to cause trouble.'

Their pleas were ignored.

'They were told to piss off because they'd had their chance,' the officer said.

'It was too late. It's the first time I have seen 35 guys crying like babies. Some of them actually shit their pants. Seriously, they crapped all over themselves.'

With the inmates, sad and sorry, sitting behind bars, the clean-up began.

'It looked like a war zone,' said the officer. 'There was shit everywhere.' There were also weapons. 'We found about a dozen shivs in the Muslim Yard. And these were not shivs you could just knock up in the spur of the moment. These had thought and effort put into them, and it was a pretty big indication the Muslim Yard was planning to riot. It could have been a whole lot worse, and there is no doubt it was planned – the barbecue was just an excuse.'

Fifteen men were charged with rioting, and several officers were given bravery medals for the courage they showed on the day.

Was this a minor incident? Absolutely not. Was it religiously motivated?

'Yeah, there were Muslim screams,' the officer said. 'They were yelling *Allahu akbar*, and the rear teams were getting threats. They were saying they would execute their families, chop off their heads and post it on YouTube. There were blokes praying before we went in, stuff like that, so there was certainly a religious element. But, really, they rioted because they wanted to. The animals just wanted to go wild.'

5

SUPERMAX

Dry, Flaky Skin

To whom it may concern,

We of the HRMU [High-Risk Management Unit] are writing this letter in a last-ditch effort to have the allegations regarding mental and physical abuse investigated by an independent body before the damage inflicted upon us by this regime is irreversible. There is no fresh air, there is no natural light, and our reading material is sometimes removed for months. Visits are cancelled with no justification, and under-age visitors are being subjected to unreasonable and illegal strip searches. The air-conditioning is constantly set on cold throughout winter when the temperature is already below zero, and the stale air causes dry, flaky skin. Safe cells are used as a form of torture, and many inmates have been placed there on the justification that they threatened self-harm. Once in there, they have headbutted walls for hours on end or punched at the door, clearly in a state of distress. They have been left in there to make fools of themselves for the officers' personal amusement. These cells are the equivalent to the cool rooms used by the Nazis as torture during World War II.

Yours sincerely,

Lindsay Rose, Ronald Priestly, Rabeeh Mawas, Leith Merchant, Konstantinos Georgiou and Dudley Aslett.

This is a condensed version of the letter a group of men serving a total of seven life sentences plus 137 years smuggled out of Goulburn Jail in 2007 to complain about, among other things, brown bread, small underwear, green fruit and cold meals served in the prison they call Supermax – a 75-cell 'jail within a jail' that holds the worst prisoners in the country.

The first batch of inmates included gang rapists, psychopaths and men like Ivan Milat, the serial killer who murdered seven backpackers and has spent his whole time in prison both plotting to escape and mutilating himself.

'They were not impulsive hotheads but cold planners of violence,' former Corrective Services Commissioner Ron Woodham said, 'some of whom have no respect for law enforcement and, in some cases, no respect for human life. We needed somewhere to put them where they could no longer harm others.'

'I worked in there for 18 months,' said former Supermax guard Kevin Camberwell. 'The original concept of the place was just to house inmates that were a problem in all the other jails. Before 2001, all the tracs [intractables] were skipped around the country. They dealt with them by never allowing them to settle. But it didn't really work, so they built the Supermax to house them all in one place, but now it has grown to become a dumping ground for terrorists who are classified as AA inmates.'

With a price tag of $22 million, the Supermax prison was the culmination of a four-year planning process prompted by the Killing Fields. Former New South Wales premier Bob Carr opened the facility on a crisp winter's morning in June 2001, but not without controversy.

'It's not an electronic zoo like Katingal,' Ron Woodham said, referring to the last purpose-built Supermax-type prison within the Long Bay Jail complex. Katingal was closed in 1978 after recommendations from the Royal Commission into New South Wales Prisons. 'There is no sensory deprivation. And the prisoners won't get bashed like they did in Grafton Jail [during the period when it housed the most intractable prisoners]. There are no tiger cages – the solid steel cells they had in the front yards of Goulburn Jail – and the jail can be run as a tight or a relaxed regime, although both will be secure.'

But Carr was forced to issue a dare to opposition MP Andrew Humpherson, who felt the facility more closely resembled a luxury hotel: 'Anyone who's silly enough to say this is five-star accommodation, we'll book you in for a week, but only when the interesting guests are here as well.'

Humpherson had criticised the Supermax facilities for including basketball and tennis courts, TVs, microwaves, toasters, an outdoor walking track and a personal counsellor.

And yet Milat and his men *complained*? Letters about overripe fruit? Brown bread? Dry, flaky skin?

Cry me a river.

The Harm(U)

Officially called the High-Risk Management Unit (HRMU) when it opened, and later the High-Risk Management Correctional Centre (HRMCC), Goulburn's Supermax prison is not the type of facility that strikes fear into the heart of a criminal. In fact, the prison, with its cream walls, kitchens and gardens, looks more like a clinic than an institution of punishment for Australia's worst men.

'It was all pretty modern and nice to look at, a self-unit type thing where they had their own kitchen and yard. The cells are extremely clean; nothing is grim,' said former Goulburn supervisor Dave Farrell. 'When people build a jail they think it needs to be stark and horrible, but that is not the case. You need to think about the staff who are going to work in the building. They need to work in a nice place because they are not working with nice people. The aim in building a place like this isn't to punish the inmates; it's to control them. They have established themselves as the most difficult inmates in the state, and the building is about making them as easy as possible to manage. They are not going to be rehabilitated or let out, so you are just putting them in an environment where they can't kill any other inmates or staff.

'The HRMU gave us better control. A lot of thought went into it and the design. The structure and policy of the place gives staff and management greater control when it comes to prisoner movement. Prisoners are restricted in associations, moved under heavy escort, and they spend a lot of time on their own. But they are also given enough to keep them moderately happy. You have to make sure you give them the prospect of reward and access to things that they can enjoy in their daily life. It's all very good and well to say, "Throw them in a hole and feed them meals," but what happens to the person who has to bring them their meal when the prisoner is mad as hell?'

But don't be fooled by fresh paint and kitchenettes. As Bob Carr said, this ain't no resort. Supermax is situated on a third-of-a-kilometre square plot on the north-west corner of the Goulburn Jail complex. Inmates would have a nice view over the historic town if it wasn't for the almost impenetrable and windowless white masonry walls lined by five-metre-high fences topped with razor wire.

'And then there is the eight-metre exclusion zone that is guarded by officers with high-powered rifles and state-of-the-art video surveillance,' said a current Supermax guard. 'And the two towers that overlook it, and also the six-metre outer-wall. There would be a nice view, but these blokes will never see it. They are not getting out of here.'

While the officers in the two towers might not always be looking, the cameras are. The 24-hour surveillance includes a camera mounted on the top of a 12-metre pole looking down at all that moves on the ground, and there is another pointing towards the sky, just in case anyone is thinking of hijacking a helicopter and trying a Silverwater-type John Killick escape.

Inside, things are certainly sterile but not serene. Inmates spend most of the day locked inside a two by three metre cell that is completely bare except for a toilet, a shower (to prevent them from stabbing each other to death), a bed and a little table, all of which are fixed to either the walls or floor. The bed is a concrete slab with a not-so-comfortable but fireproof 25-centimetre-thick piece of foam that serves as a mattress. Each inmate lives alone in his cell – or 'one-out', in jail speak – and, depending on their behaviour, they have access to a kitchenette and a 250-square-metre grassed exercise yard, all green except for the striking orange of the looping running track.

'The cells are all one-out, but they have their own day room,' said Kevin Camberwell. 'The day room is connected to two, three or four cells, depending on what stage or program the [prisoner is] in. The whole system is set up into stages. They will start in segregation for 21 days and then progress to another section from there, and so on. The inmates in those cells will share that one day room, although they may never see each other because they are given access at different times. They have a toaster and a kettle in that day room; that is where Ivan Milat likes to spend most of his time.'

This system of rewards gives prisoners access to basic kitchen appliances and TVs if they behave and progress through the prison program. And those things are taken

100

away if they regress. Food, of course, cannot be taken away . . . even if it is sometimes overripe.

'Breakfast was at 8am,' said Camberwell of the day's first meal, after it has been X-rayed. 'All their meals were delivered to them in their cells. Lunch was at 11am and dinner at 4pm. They couldn't choose their food. The only exceptions were made for allergies or a religious diet, like halal meats for the Muslims. They just got whatever was on the menu that day. It was normal stuff, like sausage and vegies, chops, potatoes. Sometimes they would get a full piece of steak; other times it would be curries or stews.'

The Supermax inmates, who have killed more than 40 people between them, also get pizza, spinach-and-ricotta burgers, Streets Blue Ribbon ice-cream, Tim Tams and popcorn.

'It was pretty good food, actually,' Camberwell continued. 'And they could use their buy-up to purchase soft drink. They had coffee and tea provided; it was rationed every day. They also had a fridge in the day room. They would label their drinks if it was shared with any other inmates. Most of the time it didn't create difficulties. You wouldn't sip out of a can marked "Ivan Milat", would you?'

Inmates in Supermax are given a packet of breakfast cereal, 300 millilitres of milk, seven slices of bread, coffee, tea and sugar each morning. For lunch they get sandwiches – turkey, chicken and mayo, lettuce, cranberry and ham, roast beef . . . pretty much whatever they fancy – served with fruit and a side of yoghurt. So again, Ivan . . .

Cry me a river.

Surprisingly, inmates wear white – no prison green, none of the bright-orange jumpsuits popularised by TV.

'They only wear the orange when they are going on visits or escorts,' Camberwell explained. 'Orange is for extreme high-risk inmates in general population, so you would know to keep an eye on them. They wear white overalls the rest of the time.

'They all wore the same thing, and everything they had was given to them by us. As they progressed through different sections they got things, even their own shoes and clothes.'

Some residents are allowed to associate with other inmates, but most lead a lonely existence, their best friend a toaster or a TV. Camberwell went on to describe a typical day in Supermax:

'They don't spend much time out of their cells. And it really depends on who it is and how they behave. They are out of their cells in the morning after breakfast and a security check. They are left in their own yard to do as they please. The yard is outside their cell, but it is most certainly not a football yard or a botanic garden. It's about ten foot by eight foot and completely bare. They would either spend the morning in there or in the day room if they were allowed.'

The behaviour-based system also determines how much time they spend out of their cells, how much contact they are allowed to have with other inmates, and when, how often and from whom they can receive visits.

'At this present stage all the cells are full,' Camberwell said. 'Supermax is set up in a way that you can just lock them in their cell and leave them there all day if they don't behave. There is no reason they need to come out, but they can if they earn the right.

'We chose [which other inmates] they associated with if they'd earned that privilege. We did have problems where inmates had issues with each other, and to get at each other they would ask to associate with them. They ended up punching on, so we stopped that by taking away the option of letting them choose their associations. Later we also had terrorists associating, and we would also have blokes coercing to try and change their stories for court appeals.'

Prisoners also earn the right to make phone calls – screened, of course – and they can rent things like radios and TVs, but never 'own' them.

'They had to book in for phone calls,' Camberwell continued. 'They could not have them whenever they wanted. They were all approved by the commissioner's office, so they just couldn't talk to Joe Blow. Same with their visits; they had to be approved by the commissioner's office. If they wanted to have someone visit them, they would have to apply.

'We controlled everything they had and everything they did, and it was a tactic used to keep them in line.'

Despite a list of residents that included such violent creatures as Milat, Camberwell described the jail as 'boring' – at least as far as work went.

'I was in there from 2010 until 2012,' Camberwell recalled. 'I didn't really fit in because a lot of people in there had already been working there for ten years or so. I didn't enjoy working in that jail, to be honest. Nothing much happened because of the way it was set up and the amount of control we had. I suppose you could say the prison did its job. A lot of the guards wanted to get back out into the "real" jail because there was much more action outside of Supermax.'

'Take someone like Milat,' Camberwell continued. 'His average day was completely controlled and he couldn't cause any trouble. He wouldn't associate with anybody and no one wanted anything to do with him. He was a complete loner. The only reason he would go into the common area was so that he wasn't stuck in his cell. There would never be anyone in there with him. He just read the paper, books and magazines. He was never involved in anything because wherever he went there were four staff with him and he would be handcuffed and shackled.'

Conditions were also strict for guards in a bid – a sometimes unsuccessful bid – to stop dodgy officers from smuggling in contraband.

'They have searches on staff in three separate locations before going in,' Camberwell said. 'Different people and different locations. There are also metal detectors.'

The prisoners were always watched, cameras and officers studying their every move. They had to.

'The whole [Supermax] area has its own intelligence officers,' Camberwell said. 'The cameras are in the day rooms and the external rooms, but there are none in the cells. The only cameras in cells are in the safe cells, and inmates are only put in the safe cells if they threaten to kill themselves, or we think they are going to. A lot of the guys would get in the safe cell and then use it as a bargaining tool. They would say, "Give me a TV or a radio and I will have something else to think about and I won't want to cause trouble." It was very popular around grand final and State of Origin time. Sometimes they were given a radio, sometimes a TV, just to get them out.'

Mr Milat's Mail

The officer picked up the chunky envelope addressed to the High Court of Australia.

Bit heavy for a bit of paper – better have a look.

The officer slowly, carefully sliced open the package that a Mr Ivan Milat was attempting to send to Australia's final court of appeal.

He shook the envelope over a table.

Plop.

A blood-splattered tissue hit the desk.

What do we have here?

The officer, wearing protective gloves, slowly pulled away tissue. One layer, another layer, a third.

And there it was . . .

A bloody finger inside a tissue.

Ivan Milat had cut off his finger and tried to mail it out of Supermax.

*

'Help!' the officer cried over the intercom. 'Come here. Come here *now*. I need help.'

Frantic officers burst through the door and into Milat's cell. The serial killer, now a serial self-mutilator, was sitting on the edge of the bed, his left hand holding his right.

'At first he looked calm,' an officer recalled. 'Even relaxed. But he wasn't being tough or anything like that. He was so placid because he was about to pass out. He was turning white.'

Milat pulled back the tissue, exposing a bloody stump.

He was missing the little finger on his right hand . . . from the top knuckle up.

'They get issued a BIC razor blade every week to shave. They have to hand the old one in before they get the new one,' said a Goulburn Supermax full-timer. 'The officer is supposed to check the old razor to make sure it is all there. The guys obviously didn't check to see if [Milat's] BIC still had the blade in it. They put it in the tub and just issued him with a new one.'

Milat wasn't showing great genius when he prised the steel from the shaver.

'You just break the plastic surrounds of the BIC and you produce the blade,' the veteran continued. 'It's easy to do. So he used the blade to hack into the finger, but he couldn't get through it, not all the way. What he did next was just gruesome. He got to the bone with the blade and stalled. I'm not sure if it had become too blunt or had broken, but [the razor] couldn't finish the job.'

Look away now if you are squeamish. Seriously . . . skip a par.

'So he broke the bone,' the officer continued. 'Not sure how. Maybe he jammed it into a wall and stomped on it, maybe he just snapped it with his other hand, but he broke it. It was broken most of the way through, but not all the way through.'

Enter a plastic picnic knife he had smuggled into the room . . . the kind designed to cut through a T-bone steak.

'He used that to finish the bone,' said the officer. 'He sawed his way through the rest.'

A report published in the *Sydney Morning Herald* on 27 January 2009 said the 64-year-old 'did not exhibit any signs of shock' when found by guards.

'He was nearly passed out when we got to the door,' said an officer. 'He was struggling big time. The door was open and he was sitting on the bed. He looked calm for a second, but he suddenly went lethargic and all limp. He had lost a heap of blood, but he must have drained it in the toilet or the shower because there was only a bit of blood in the room. Not as much as you would expect, and I've seen a lot worse.'

The *Herald* also reported that Milat was rushed to Goulburn Hospital, where 'medical staff were unable to say whether the severed finger, which had been placed on ice, could be saved.'

The newspaper never reported whether or not the finger was reattached.

'We were told he hardly said a word when he went to the hospital,' said an officer. 'The blokes that were there told us he had a bit of a smirk on his face because, despite the pain, he was Ivan Milat. It was an ego thing. The nurses immediately knew who he was and he got off on it. That's why he did shit like this.'

But did they save the finger?

'They didn't,' the guard said. 'They never even bothered. Why would they? It was on ice and all that, but there was no attempt. Who would want to save Ivan Milat?'

Kevin Camberwell claimed Milat chopped off his digit in a bloody bid to escape: 'He knew it was never going to get past security. All the mail coming in and out of there is screened. Of course it was found – and that is what he would have wanted. He would have been hoping he could escape while on escort to hospital.'

That was never going to happen, not with four armed, high-risk escorts transferring him to Goulburn Hospital.

'He was always faking injuries to try to get out of the High-Risk Management Correctional Centre,' said former Goulburn supervisor Dave Farrell. 'He reckoned the air-conditioning was playing up. He would claim it was poisoned and point to his head. It would be all red because he had stood rubbing it on the wall for half a day. He would say he was getting rashes and needed to move out. He would try anything and everything to get himself out. He was a serial pest.'

Another guard, who worked closely with Milat, said the finger-severing stunt was purely for attention and had nothing to do with an impossible escape attempt.

'It goes to show he is not completely insane because he buzzed up,' said the Supermax officer. 'That means he pressed the knock-up system [a prison intercom used by the inmates in case of emergency] to alert the officer in the control room that he was hurt. They alerted the security units and they went in to help him. He was found before the letter. It was all for attention. He just wanted to have a break from the normal routine and go and look into the eyes of the public when they recognised who he was.'

Camberwell said that experts had predicted Milat would hurt himself.

'The psychiatrist warned us that he would eventually start mutilating because he couldn't kill anyone,' he said. 'He killed because he was addicted to harm and mutilation, and they said he would need to fulfil that urge. In prison, in almost exclusive segregation, the only way he could do that was by hurting himself. And that is exactly what he did. He started with hunger strikes and then progressed.'

Ivan Milat is just one of the inmates held in the 75-cell prison within a prison they call Supermax.

Let's meet some more . . .

Secret Supermax Files

These are the secret files and untold stories of the Supermax Six – the first men to be sent to Goulburn's High-Risk Management Correctional Centre. The revealing case notes provide a fascinating insight into some of Australia's worst and most violent criminals. For instance, did you know that aliens regularly visit the cell of mass murderer Malcolm Baker? Did you know about serial killer Lindsay Rose's passion for prison gardening?

*

BAKER, Malcolm, DOB: 13/08/1947, received into the HRMCC on September 22, 2001
Extreme High Security: Classification A1.
Baker is currently serving six life sentences for murdering six people on the Central Coast in a 1992 shooting spree. Called the Central Coast Massacre, Baker shot dead his former girlfriend, her father, her pregnant sister and three others in a rampage across Terrigal, Bateau Bay and Wyong before surrendering to police.

'Selected as part of the first group to be placed in HRMCC', his Supermax file reads. 'High risk of conspiracy to assault, escape and hostage-taking. Paranoid and aggressive manner. Obsessed with subject of space and science, frequently referring to visitors from space. Lack of insight into own behaviour. Staff monitor him closely.'

'You won't get me!' screamed Baker, shaking his finger as he looked towards the sky. 'You won't fucking get me, and you can't make me do anything. You can't make me do nothing. NOT ME!'

His finger stopped pointing at the sky and started pointing towards his head.

'Ha, ha,' he said, now touching the crunched aluminum foil that he had fashioned into a hat – well, more of a helmet – and slapped onto his head. 'See? I'm too smart. Ha, HA. See? You won't fucking get me.'

This is how one of Australia's worst killers spends his days, walking around a segregated Supermax yard yelling at the sky.

'The meals in Supermax are served in little silver containers, a bit like those plastic containers you get Chinese in, but these are made with foil. He saves them up and scrunches them together and makes himself a little space helmet,' said a HRMCC officer. 'Like one of those things you would see in an old low-budget black-and-white space movie.'

The convicted killer of six tells Goulburn guards he is visited by aliens. They come into his cell at night. But the aliens aren't so bad – he has bigger problems than green men with big heads.

'He thinks people are trying to send him brain messages,' the officer continued. 'He swears that people are trying to control his mind, and he thinks they are doing it through the air-conditioning. Apparently [the Department of Corrective Services], the police force and the government are all out to get him. They have combined forces and put some type of microwave-based technology in the air-conditioning system. He says it is fucking with his brain, that they are trying to make him go crazy, so he wears the foil cap to stop the mind-control messages getting through.'

The foil might make him safe from the secret forces of the government. But not from other inmates . . .

SNAP!

The boot broke Baker's bone.

Snap. Snap.

Two more ribs cracked as the frothing inmate stomped on Baker's chest. The foil hat had fallen off after the first blow – a straight right that knocked him from his feet and flat onto his back.

The officers ran into the library and jumped on Martin Toki, another convicted murderer, who, according to his file, is a 'mentally unstable inmate prone to frequent and violent mood swings'.

The giant of a man, 'currently a Muslim but changes regularly between Buddhism and Christianity', threw one officer to the ground before he was swamped. He screamed and shouted as he was dragged to the floor, but Baker was silent – knocked out cold and lying in a pool of hurt.

'[Baker] was a nut case and was rarely allowed associations,' said a HRMCC officer. 'But, like any inmate, he did get associations from time to time. He only ever had one or two, and for some reason one of them was the extremely violent and unstable inmate called Toki.

'Baker lives in a one-out cell – they all do – but they have a common area connected to their cell that they can share with associates. On this day he was in the library.'

And that's where he was attacked, Toki's hands dropping hardcovers and forming rock-hard fists.

'He got bashed real bad,' the officer continued. 'I guess it was at the end of 2013. And when I say real bad, I mean real, real bad. Baker had severe injuries and was rushed to hospital. He had broken ribs, a smashed nose, cracked cheeks – and that's just the start of it. He was so bad that they couldn't treat him at Goulburn and he was rushed to Sydney for emergency treatment.'

The extent of the injuries came as no surprise, given that the attacker was a maniac who threatens to kill prison guards.

'Toki is a bad man,' the officer continued. 'He is one of the most violent inmates in the prison system. A lot of people don't realise but you get your real well-known inmates, guys like Milat, and really they are nothing more than a reputation. It's the inmates that you have never heard of that are the real bad ones, and Toki is one of them.

'Yep, this guy can rip TVs from walls and swing them around like King Kong. He held a TV over his head and threatened to smash it over a guard's head. They had to gas him and knock him over to stop him. That was in about 2008. He was a real problem because he was a big, strong Islander and hard to control. He was real dangerous and unpredictable. Over a period of time he behaved, and they signed off on an association. For whatever reason, he had an association with Baker.'

'Baker said something to piss him off,' the officer continued. (Maybe Toki didn't believe in aliens?) 'We don't know what it was, but it was enough to get him flogged. We got in there just quick enough to save his life.'

The officer said Baker has been 'quiet' since the incident. He still wears the foil, of course, but now he yells to the sky softly and refuses association requests.

FERNANDO, Vester, DOB: 05/04/1970, received into the HRMCC on September 14, 2001
Extreme High Security: Classification A1.

Fernando was sentenced to life for the rape and murder of Walgett nurse Sandra Hoare in 1994. He was sentenced to another 30 years in the stabbing death of Brendan Fernando, his cousin and accomplice in Hoare's murder, in Lithgow Jail in 1999.

'Lengthy history of violence both in community and custody,' his file states. 'Continues to be compliant with unit routine and polite to staff. Was recently involved in an argument with another inmate on the deck, but this appears to have been settled. Continues to receive positive feedback regarding his laundry sweeper duties. Very loyal to his family and keeps in contact with them through the phone. Extremely loyal to inmate Priestly.'

Fernando is almost your model Supermax inmate ... Almost.

'He doesn't do much wrong, but we found a big, dirty shiv in his cell one day,' said a HRMCC officer. 'He is a huge man with a history of violence, and he could have done a lot of damage with the weapon he had made. He was a handful back in his day but he'd really calmed down, and he was never angry unless it came to Muslims. He was one of the blokes who had converted to Islam, but for whatever reason he converted back.

'He just hates them now, and he had the shiv ready because he was paranoid the Muslims were out to get him. Let's just say he is very anti-Muslim, and only a potential problem to them.'

*

KANAAN, Michael, DOB: 23/05/1975, received into the HRMCC October 31, 2001

Extreme High Security: Classification A1.

Kanaan is serving three life sentences plus 50 years and four months without the possibility of parole for murdering three people in 1998. A university student aspiring to join the Australian Federal Police, Kanaan instead joined a brutal street gang led by Kings Cross drug dealer Danny Karam. He shot a man twice at Greenacre after a dispute over a gun in 1998 before murdering Karam two months later; the leader of 'DK's Boys' was hit by 16 bullets as he sat in his parked car. Kanaan was arrested in December 1998 after being shot two times in a Sydney shoot-out with police. He was also convicted of shooting two men dead in a drive-by at Five Dock, linked to the murder of 14-year-old Edward Lee and suspected of shooting up a police station.

'Received from ICMU on commissioning of the HRMCC,' his file said. 'Claimed to be a paraplegic during remand period. He has a capacity to mount an escape and has used a mobile phone whilst in jail. Noted as compliant with unit routine and polite in his interactions with staff. Kanaan rarely has contact with his counsellor as he states he is always busy training, which is his main interest now. Low-need inmate.'

It was a miracle . . .

'He just stood up and walked,' said a former prison guard. 'He rose from the wheelchair, pushed it away, and he was cured.'

Michael Kanaan – a gangster, a killer and a cop-shooting drug dealer – had been touched by the hand of God. Rendered a self-diagnosed paraplegic after going down in a hail of bullets in an infamous Sydney shoot-out with police at White City in 1998, Kanaan simply pushed his wheelchair away and walked.

'Yep, right after his trial finished,' the officer said. 'And after he knew he was safe in prison from being raped or bashed by other inmates.'

Some people even felt sorry for the master manipulator, whose ambition saw him attempt to seize control of the Kings Cross drug trade when he was just five years out of school. *But didn't he go to that good Christian school? Wasn't he going to go to university? Doesn't he have that nice family?*

That's what some thought, and maybe still think.

'Kanaan is as dangerous as he's ever been,' said a current Goulburn officer. 'He has heaps of dramas and is a bloke who will just snap. He hasn't been in a wheelchair since he was in remand – I have never seen him in a wheelchair at all. It was just a play for sympathy from the court and to stay away from the heavies when he came in, until he had it all figured out.'

Kanaan is no cripple.

'He is a fitness fanatic,' the guard said. 'He spends most of his time working out, whether out in the yard or in the cell. There are no free weights or anything like that in Supermax, but there is a chin-up bar and a dip bar.'

Up down, up down.

That's how Kanaan spends his days. Chin-ups and dips outside, push-ups and sit-ups in his cell.

Up down, up down.

'He has the strongest back I've seen,' said the guard. 'It is massive. He is a strong little fucker. He has thrown a few guards off that fucking back, let me tell you.'

Have you heard the one about the triple homicide convict being allowed out of Australia's most secure prison for a consultation with a plastic surgeon? The inmate who sat in the high-profile Sydney hospital wanting the scars left by police-issue bullets to be removed?

No? Well, read on.

'[Kanaan] is pretty vain,' the officer continued. 'And for some reason we can't work out what genius decided they would let him go and get some plastic surgery. This wasn't anything to do with his health. It was purely cosmetic because he thought the scars were ugly. Thankfully, the department was not going to pay for it. He had the money to get it done himself, and he was taken down to Sydney to have the surgery.'

Unfortunately, the world-renowned surgeon had bad news, and, apparently, Kanaan does not like bad news . . .

'He was told nothing could be done about the scars because of some skin condition or something,' the officer said. 'So he exploded and tried to belt the doctor, and he would have had he not been restrained by the guards that were escorting him.'

Kanaan's case notes, however, are complimentary. He is described as a polite and obedient inmate.

'He is fine until he gets the wrong answer,' the officer said. 'And that's when he snaps. He can be massive trouble. He is fine if he gets his visits, his calls and his associations, but you have a big problem if you tell him no. He tries to be smart and cunning, but we have a handle on him. We've seen him at his worst, and we know exactly how to deal with him. But he is a dangerous inmate. He has access to a lot of money and is still connected both inside and out. There's a reason he's in Supermax and a reason why he will never get out.'

PUAFISI, Fisatina, DOB: 22/09/1972, received into the HRMCC on September 15, 2001
Extreme High Security: Classification E1
A Supermax original, Puafisi was released in 2006 after serving a sentence for maliciously inflicting grievous bodily harm and assaulting an officer.

'Left HRMCC to freedom on 07/02/06 and ten months later returned to custody after stabbing a security guard 30 times,' his file reads. 'Diagnosed with mental illness and adjustment dependent on medication compliance. Known to go off medication and to descend into violence.'

The security guard was busting. Too much water and too many people had him knocking down doors and ripping at his zipper – it was almost Christmas and Campbelltown Mall was packed.

'Ahhhh,' he sighed in relief. 'Finally.'

The 38-year-old guard had asked for his toilet break four times.

'Nup,' the reply came. 'Too busy. It's Christmas. You can wait.'

But he was *busting*.

'Okay,' the boss said. 'Be quick.'

But he never came back . . .

Pop. Pop. Pop.

He sprayed the wall with piss as he spun around.

Pop. Pop. Pop. Pop. Pop.

He swung but it was too late – the ten-centimetre paring knife had already ripped him apart.

'From our information, the security guard was just using the toilet,' recalled Campbelltown police inspector Michael Cook. 'There was no verbal exchange at all. Absolutely none. It was just one of those crazy things. [Puafisi] punctured a lung and stabbed him in the heart. No provocation. No demands. Very strange.'

The toilet was packed with men dragged to the mall by their Christmas-shopping better halves, so there were several witnesses to the attack.

'It is just as well we got him,' the inspector said. 'He is a very dangerous man.'

The bloodied guard was rushed to Liverpool Hospital for emergency surgery on his 30 wounds. He lived, thankfully, but only because Puafisi shoplifted an easily pocketed paring knife instead of something bigger.

Police were tipped off – a big bloke was running around covered in blood and issuing threats. The 34-year-old suspect was soon arrested at a scrubland campsite in nearby Ruse. The inspector brought up his file once he had him cuffed and calm, quietly curled up in a cell.

And then it all made sense.

'He had just been let out of Supermax,' recalled a current HRMCC officer. 'In fact, he is the only guy I know of that has ever been released from the HRMCC – and boy was that a mistake. He was out for a while, but it was only a matter of time. Mad Eyes, that's what we call him, had stolen something and he got paranoid. He thought a security guard was looking at him. So he went and stole a knife and watched the guard. He stalked him for a while, and then he got his chance when [the guard] left to go to the toilet. Pua just followed him in and stabbed the shit out of him.'

Officers who have worked with 'Mad Eyes' question the sensibility of his 2006 release.

'He has scared a lot of people in prison,' said an unnamed officer. 'He is big, he is crazy, and he is strong. He is obviously mad, but I guess he's okay when he's on his meds. But fuck me . . . You don't want to cross him if he forgets to take a pill.'

ROSE, Lindsay, DOB: 02/05/1955, received into the HRMCC on September 14, 2001
Extreme High Security: Classification A1
Rose is a convicted serial killer sentenced to five consecutive

life sentences without the possibility of parole. He was found guilty of murdering five people between 1984 and 1994.

'Murder times five,' Rose's file reads. 'Cold-blooded murders. Intelligent and educated. He is capable of manipulative behaviour, particularly to remain in the HRMCC. Allegedly plotted to escape from Long Bay involving the murder of a staff member. Known to produce gaol-made keys. He is a high risk of escape . . . He continues to access the running track area regularly so he can maintain the garden area. Sees his counsellor for support issues only.'

Poetic is a man called Rose becoming a gardener. Poetic justice is a five-time cold-blooded killer ending up with horrible haemorrhoids. Yep, serial killer Lindsay Rose was noted as an 'intelligent and educated' man who spent his time 'maintaining' the Supermax garden. He was paid $12 a week to weed and water. He was happy . . . until he got haemorrhoids.

'He was moved to Long Bay because he got horrible haemorrhoids,' said an officer well known to Rose. 'Not just "ouch" haemorrhoids but the type that sends you permanently into a bed.'

Rose, who shot Fatma Ozonal in a massage parlour before stabbing former girlfriend Kerrie Pang to death as part of a contract killing in Gladesville in 1994, is no longer in Supermax. He is in Long Bay Prison hospital with a very sore arse.

'He needed to get full-time care,' said a guard. 'He had a very bad problem.'

Officers described Rose as a hard worker, who always had the best prison jobs because he was a police informant.

'He is a massive *Dog*,' said another Goulburn officer. 'He is always going to see police, telling them what he knows. He is constantly going on about Ivan Milat, claiming he knows where his second burial ground is.

'He always did the gardening wherever he was. He did that because it was a job and he got paid well. In truth, he was a disgusting human being but a good inmate. He was a good worker, polite and easy to deal with. He now has a real problem with the new generation of inmates because they don't know who he is and they don't fear him. He thinks he should be respected because he is high profile.'

MILAT, Ivan, DOB: 22/12/1944, received into the HRMCC on September 14, 2001
Extreme High Security: Classification A1.
A serial killer known as the 'Backpacker Murderer', Milat is serving seven consecutive life sentences plus 18 years without the possibility of parole for murdering seven people. Aged between 19 and 22, the victims were found in the Belanglo State Forest, near Berrima, in New South Wales. Milat, a road worker at the time, was arrested in 1994.

'Attempted to escape from Maitland,' his file reads. 'He is a self-harm risk and serial appellant and complainant. High risk of instrumental self-harm via hunger strike if things don't go his way. No evidence of mental illness or disorder. He is noted as compliant with unit routine and polite in his interactions with staff. Milat continues to see his counsellor regularly, and he's been taking all of his meals. Staff reports he does a good job as unit sweeper.'

Milat doesn't seem concerned about ditching the digit, the one the not-so-concerned surgeons never intended to sew back on.

'I don't regret it, though it was a stupid act,' Milat said in a letter to his brother Bill Milat, dated 2 February.

A ridiculous thing to do, but in here acts like that *are* regarded as normal and really not as severe as some. I wonder if I will have enough time to prove my innocence as time flies, but it takes a long time to get a reply from the authority-courts-government. That was a big factor in severing the finger off, to highlight the difficulties of a prisoner who wishes to appeal his case.

The prison controllers seem to think I need some punishment, so they took my plastic plates and cup, and my main meal in a sealed pack is tipped out on a dinner plate, no means given to cut anything up, and I never eat tea at 2 to 2.15 [when they deliver it].

So by the time I do feel like eating at 6 or 6.30, odd, it's a soggy, cold mess. And they took my Breville away. I always rely on that, use it to reheat, cook other things, even to toast bread.

Unfortunately for the men who guard him, Mr Milat's bloody mail is only one of his many mischievous misdemeanors.

'He needs constant supervision and will try anything for attention,' said a current HRMCC officer. 'He is famous for it. He can complain all he wants, but the extra attention he receives is warranted.'

Let's take a look at some of the other things he has done to warrant soggy meals and a ban on toasted cheese . . .

The doctor slipped the X-ray into the metal slot before flicking on the fluorescent light.

'Unbelievable,' he said, pointing to the illuminated black-and-white film. 'Would you take a look at that. Looks like a razor blade.' He leaned in closer. 'Yep – it is. And there's another one. And another one.'

But that wasn't all that was in Ivan Milat's gut. The doctor continued to point at the film, more humoured than horrified.

'That seems to be a nail clipper chain,' he continued. 'And those are staples. It would appear there are 24 in total.'

As a result of this first truly bizarre and sickening stunt in 2001, Milat was found in crippling pain and immediately taken to hospital to have the stationery items removed.

'He did it as a protest to Goulburn,' said an officer. 'He just hated it there.'

Milat was first moved to the jail that he compared to the 'Bronx' in another one of his intercepted letters in 1997, when authorities learned he was plotting to escape from Maitland Jail with notorious inmate George Savvas (more on him later). The duo was planning on beating up guards, stealing their uniforms and scaling the prison walls.

So Milat was sent to Goulburn, where officers would squeeze his toothpaste out of its tube several times a week, run metal detectors over his clothes and poke holes through his soap. It was during one of those regular cell searches that guards uncovered a hacksaw blade hidden in a packet of biscuits.

'It was a tiny blade,' said a Goulburn officer. 'And he never had a chance to use it. The bars were all intact and the blade was taken.'

It can be revealed here, for the first time, that Milat was not alone in this biscuit blade escape bid.

'The guy that helped him was the bloke that bashed a lady in Kings Cross,' said an officer. 'His name was Thomas Wilson Hudson. He was a bouncer at the time of the attack, and he'd assaulted a woman before putting her in a 44-gallon drum. He thought he had killed her but the lady survived, and she had no trouble identifying him because Hudson is a bit of a genetic freak in that he can't grow any hair on his body. He can't grow *anything*, and his lack of eyebrows, eyelashes, head hair, face hair . . . well, you know what I'm saying . . . That's what got him busted.

'Anyway, he was another one in Goulburn, and him and Milat became tight. They had the escape all planned together in the MPU, but they got busted. He was Milat's offsider for a while, and he was a real dangerous bloke. He had to be moved around Goulburn Jail because he was so dangerous. He was into his martial arts and fitness, and he ended up being deported back to New Zealand because he was too much trouble.'

Hudson got deported and Ivan got moved. *Constantly.* And he got searched. *All the time.*

'That's why he started with the self-harm,' another officer said. 'He thought he would be moved to another jail after he swallowed the razors.'

But he wasn't. And what came next was truly bizarre, even for a man who snacks on staples . . .

Milat lodged a complaint to the Information and Privacy Commission New South Wales, claiming his rights had been violated after his X-rays were publicly released and published by media outlets. He demanded up to $40,000 in compensation. The Hon. Charlie Lynn had this to say about the letter in a sitting of the New South Wales parliament:

> I wish to comment on a recent report that serial psychopath Ivan Milat has appealed to the New South Wales Privacy Commissioner, Mr Chris Puplick, to investigate a complaint regarding the public release of X-rays taken when he swallowed three razor blades, 24 staples and a nail clipper chain when he was in solitary confinement in Goulburn Gaol. Milat claimed that this was a breach of his privacy. I understand that Milat's claim was rejected by the ombudsman. However, it has been taken up by the New South Wales Privacy Commissioner. If the complaint is accepted, I understand that Milat will be in the running for up to $40,000 in compensation.
>
> I understand that Milat is currently detained in Supermax, a 70-bed, high-risk management unit within

Goulburn Gaol. I also understand that authorities within the prison system believe that Milat's stunt in swallowing the razor blades, staples and nail clippers was staged to force his transfer to a lower security prison. The editorial in the *Daily Telegraph* of 31 October got it right when it suggested that if there were to be any inquiry at all into this matter, it should be conducted within the prison system to establish how an inmate, such as Milat, obtained razor blades and the other paraphernalia he swallowed.

The editorial also reminded us of the case last month of the convicted rapist Bilal Skaf. Mr Puplick's office was of the view that his parents, if not Skaf himself, could be eligible for a similar level of compensation over the release of security camera footage of an attempt to smuggle letters out of prison. Chris Puplick believes that criminals like Ivan Milat and Bilal Skaf have a right to privacy. In Milat's case, he has suggested that any pressure applied to his office to reject Milat's claim could amount to corruption under the *Independent Commission Against Corruption Act*. If this is the case, we need to advise the New South Wales Privacy commissioner that he is totally out of touch with community expectations. We also need to change the *ICAC Act* to ensure that it cannot be manipulated by misguided serial do-gooders.

Ivan Milat forfeited any right he had to ever see the light of day when he was convicted of the premeditated, cold-blooded murder of seven backpackers. The only right he has is to a jug of water, a slice of bread and a bowl of rice in a small, dark cell every day for the rest of his miserable life.

Water, bread and rice – how about a PlayStation then? Milat's next stunt was to go on a nine-day hunger strike after his requests to have a PlayStation put in his cell were refused. Milat said he required the gaming console to 'exercise his mind', and he refused all meals over a nine-day period in protest. He dropped 25kg in little over a week, going from 85kg to 60kg.

'There's no inmate on my watch who would ever get anything close to a PlayStation, particularly Australia's worst serial killer,' said then prison boss Ron Woodham. 'I knew he'd start eating again because he likes his food too much. He can stage as many protests as he likes, but there'd be no point if he got one because he needs two hands to use it.'

Milat was carefully monitored throughout his hunger strike, with medics and prison staff on hand and ready to administer food intravenously to prevent Milat from dying in custody.

Milat has been involved in several other protests while incarcerated in Goulburn; one saw him again refuse to eat because his television reception was fuzzy. He also slammed his hand into a door and required 24 stiches in another painful bid to get out of Goulburn.

Just like its predecessor, the infamous Katingal – the Long Bay Jail Supermax that was razed to the ground after its barbaric practices were revealed – the HRMCC is not without controversy or critics.

Former Head of Corrections Tony Vinson believes the jail should not be used as a long-term solution for problematic inmates.

'I criticised Mr Carr publicly at the time he opened it,' Vinson, now a University of Sydney professor, said. 'When he opened it, Mr Carr said, "We are going to brick them in." To protect a prison officer's life or someone else's life, it may be required to do something like this on the short-term. As an enduring solution it strokes the sentiments of politicians, the sentiments of all those people who claim they have brought it upon themselves. It is far better to disperse these inmates across the system. It's a theatre stage. The rationale for having large prison populations is that people sleep better at night. That is the lie of it all. The use of a Supermax on this basis is wrong, and the nature of the offence rather than a judgment of the individual is also wrong.'

Former NSW Council for Civil Liberties president Cameron Murphy went as far as calling on the United Nations to shut down the prison he compared to the Guantanamo Bay detention camp, the infamous US 'black site' where the protections of the Geneva Convention were ignored.

Murphy called conditions at the southern New South Wales prison both cruel and degrading. He called on the UN's Special Rapporteur on Torture to visit the facility in the council's Shadow Report on Australia and Torture.

'Prisoners are kept in cells that measure two by three metres for 22 hours or more a day,' said council president

Murphy. 'When an inmate enters the HRMU, they are kept in segregation for as long as two weeks. This is having a significant impact on the mental health of inmates.

'Article 16 of the convention against torture prohibits cruel, inhuman or degrading treatment or punishment. The NSW Council for Civil Liberties is concerned that conditions at the HRMU violate the convention against torture.'

Murphy also recommended that the UN meet with the human rights commissioner and the NSW ombudsman.

Murphy said the council had 'made a mockery' of the UN's Special Rapporteur on Torture by calling on them to investigate the Supermax facility.

The UN never investigated the prison; MPs declared the council's request ludicrous and a play for headlines.

And maybe it was.

Now a member of the Australian Labor Party vying for a seat in the Division of Banks in Sydney's south-west, Mr Murphy did not seem so passionate about the issue when contacted for this book. He refused to comment about the subject he was so eager to pursue while in his former role.

Maybe defending Australia's worst prisoners is not a good move for a politician wanting votes?

6

TERROR

Mobile Horror
14 February 2015

The mobile phone was found under the bed.

'What do we have here?' asked the officer as he searched the inmate's cell after an intelligence tip-off. 'Nice little phone, hey? He won't be calling Mummy tonight.'

A SIM card and an SD (Secure Digital) card were also seized from the cell, located in the Lebanese Wing of the racially segregated Goulburn Jail.

No one was surprised or shocked by the find.

Just another mobile phone, they thought . . . at least until they saw what was on it.

'It was hardcore ISIS [Islamic State of Iraq and Syria] material,' said an officer who asked to remain anonymous. 'Beheading videos and full-on jihadist stuff.'

Details of the find, which sent a terror shockwave through the prison and further heightened concerns that the prison is becoming a terrorist breeding ground, can be revealed for the first time.

'It was absolutely shocking,' said the officer. 'We have never had anything like that in the prison before. Terror is a problem in prison, but we never thought they would be getting stuff like this – it's a bloody worry. Just who sent it in to them? *Why* did they send it to them? This is serious stuff.'

Goulburn Jail is officially on terror alert with hardcore Muslims suspected of waging jihad from behind bars. Intelligence files are kept on several Islamic inmates. Their mail is screened, their phone calls are monitored, and the gathered information is sent to Australia's peak terror-fighting body, ASIO (Australian Security Intelligence Organisation).

'It's a real big thing for CIG [Corrections Intelligence Group] at the moment,' revealed another officer. 'The group's time is split between gathering intelligence on outlaw motorcycle clubs and Islamic inmates. There is a feeling around that [an act of terror] could be plotted in prison. A feeling that something big could happen. They are getting more brazen overseas, and we have a microcosm of that community in this prison.'

The officer said most Muslim inmates in Goulburn Jail are kept up to date with the activities of terrorists through easily accessible and legal media.

'They are getting information through TVs, radios and newspapers,' he said. 'They know it's escalating outside, and a lot of them want to be involved.'

ASIO has a special interest in Goulburn Jail with the prison home to convicted terrorists, including Khaled Cheikho, Moustafa Cheikho, Mohamed Ali Elomar, Abdul Rakib Hasan and Mohammed Omar Jamal. Labelled the 'Terror Five', these men were sentenced to a maximum of 28 years for plotting a series of terror attacks across Sydney. They were among the first to be charged with hardline anti-terror legislation introduced following the 2001 terrorist attack on the World Trade Center in New York.

'Information is found in letters all the time,' said the officer. 'It is gathered from Intel and sent to ASIO. ASIO is across everything that happens here, and they have a lot of contact with us because of who we have and what they are doing.'

Aside from harbouring Australia's worst terrorists in our equivalent to Guantanamo, Goulburn also faces a unique problem caused by the prison's controversial policy of racial segregation.

'Most of the Muslims are grouped together in the one yard,' the officer said. 'The Lebanese Yard is completely Islamic. They don't have to go far to find a like-minded individual, and there is little doubt it makes it easier for certain individuals to share their extremist ideals.'

The situation has become so serious that convicts are being searched for any signs or clues in a bid to help identify possible extremists within the New South Wales Corrections system.

'At the moment they have us taking photos of tattoos,' said an officer, who asked to remain anonymous. 'We take photos of pictures, letters, tattoos. When we strip search them, if there is anything out of the ordinary or ISIS related, we take pictures and send them to the investigations unit. They get the ISIS flag tattooed, things like that.

'It's a worry – a massive worry – and there has been heavy training to deal with the problem over the last 18 months.'

Welcome to a world of secret codes and listening devices, of prison conversions and prayer groups, of terrorists and spies.

The Recruiter

He strokes his beard as he looks through the fence. He scans the yard.

Him. Maybe him. Yeah, he should be easy.

His target is now firmly in his sights. *Locked and loaded.*

'Over here, my brother,' he fires, his voice easily carrying across the 15-metre divide that separates the Lebanese Yard from the Koori Yard. 'Come speak with me. Come speak with Allah.'

The Indigenous inmate is soon listening intently; his hands are full of wire fence and his ears are full of the Word of God. The bearded man speaks of virgins, paradise and what happens to those committed to jihad.

Come join us. Virgins. Paradise. Jihad.

Soon the Indigenous prisoner is in a Friday prayer group . . .

A self-styled sheikh, jailed for whipping a man 40 times with an electric cord for breaking sharia law, Wassim Fayad has been placed on an ASIO watchlist because of his relentless – and successful – bid to convert Goulburn inmates to Islam.

He is one of several prisoners placed under surveillance by the CIG because of terror suspicions. Let's find out why . . .

Cristian Martinez wanted help.

'It means I am going to tie you up, brother,' said Fayad, the man Martinez had sought out for guidance as he battled drug addiction. 'That's what you need.'

Three men, Fayad's devoted followers, grabbed Martinez and pushed him into his bed. The religious outlaws had forced their way into the 32-year-old's Silverwater home sometime after midnight on 17 July 2011.

Whack.

An electric cord smashed into his bare skin, leaving a rising red snake on his back.

Whack. Whack. Whack.

The red welt continued to grow.

Whack. Whack. Whack. Whack.

Soon there was blood, the relentless plastic cord slicing through skin.

'Stop!' the victim cried. 'No more. Stop. *Pleeeeaseee.*'

Whack. Whack. Whack. Whack. Whack.

'This is for your own good,' the reply came after another five slaps.

Fayad had worked himself into a frenzy. He whipped Martinez 40 times in total, leaving Martinez bleeding, bruised and in agony for a week – the man he was supposed to be helping.

Fayad was one of four men arrested for the assault. They claimed they had punished the man after one of the alleged attackers – Zakaryah Raad – had attended Martinez's unit block in the hours proceeding the attack and saw 'beer bottles strewn throughout the premises'.

Fayad claimed Martinez had broken sharia law, the moral code and religious law of Islam, by consuming alcohol. The whipping was his punishment – his *lawful* punishment.

Sydney magistrate Brian Maloney disagreed. 'It was never about the Islamic faith or Islamic law,' he said. 'And my findings bear witness to the fact. It was simply one man who happened to be Muslim, assaulting another man, to effect a criminal purpose. To assist in that purpose, [Fayad] recruited three young men who had been groomed and duped into believing he was righteous and learned in Islamic law.'

Maloney said Fayad had whipped Martinez because of unpaid debts.

'Mr Fayad,' the magistrate said, looking directly at the accused before sentencing him to a minimum jail term of 16 months, 'by your actions you have brought much shame on the Islamic faith. You have proved yourself unscrupulously cunning, deceptive and dishonest. You profess to be a religious man, however, you resorted to violence upon Mr Martinez.'

Fayad was already a man of interest to counterterrorism police. He called Sydney's *Sunday Telegraph* in 2011 and told a reporter that 9/11 mastermind Osama bin Laden had 'died a martyr'. He was then one of two central leaders in a Sydney CBD riot later that year but, to his credit, he worked with police to quell the angry crowd.

Fayad was granted bail in 2013 after appealing his sentence for assaulting Martinez. And that's when counter-terrorism police swooped . . .

Fayad was arrested after a seven-month investigation that attempted to establish links between the 'sheikh' and a syndicate sending young Muslims to fight in Syria, and a failed ram raid on an ATM machine in northern Sydney. Counterintelligence police led the investigation because they suspected the proceeds of the crime would have been used to fund terror. The Counter Terrorism and Special Tactics Command charged Fayed with aggravated break and enter. He was also facing a separate charge of accessory after the fact in an unrelated murder case. Needless to say, his bail was revoked, and Fayad was sent to prison. To Goulburn, of course . . .

'There are lots of inmates converting to Islam,' said a current serving officer close to the intelligence program. 'And Fayad is in the middle of it. Three-quarters of the guys in the Aboriginal Yard would now be Muslim, by my estimate. They are the group mainly being targeted for conversion, partly because they are next to the Muslim Yard; they are considered easy to bring into the fold because of their history of persecution.

'Fayad is well known to the CIG. When he first came to jail the officers were really worried about him. They didn't want to put him in with the Muslim inmates because they were worried he was too extreme and would lead them into fundamentalism.

'The boss had intel that when he came through the MRRC [Metropolitan Remand and Reception Centre at Silverwater] he had already tried to convert a lot of inmates. He's very charismatic and also, we believe, radical. He will try and convert anyone.'

Fayad was first kept in segregation from the Muslim majority in the Lebanese Yard so, wait for it . . . he wouldn't convert anyone.

'They put him in D Wing at first,' the officer continued. 'It was the next wing away from the Muslims, and it was soon realised to be a very dumb move. Put it this way: there were a lot of people to convert in that yard! Common sense soon prevailed and he was put in the Muslim Yard where there weren't any non-Muslims to convert.'

But he didn't give up.

What, a fence? Is it soundproof?

'He spent all of his days talking through the fence to the other yards,' the officer continued. 'It's easy to hold conversations through the gap we walk through, because it's only about 15 metres.'

There is nothing wrong with attempting, or succeeding, to convert someone to Islam. Every Australian has the right to both choose and preach their religion. In fact, becoming a devout Muslim is, in this author's opinion, a good thing for inmates, provided they are not led down a radical path.

'The issue is that he is suspected of recruiting them for jihad,' the officer continued. 'For example, one of his sidekicks came out and was talking to one of the officers recently. He was a Muslim bloke, and he described some of the recent converts as dumb-monkey bomb-chuckers. That's what he said about the Aboriginals. He said they were being converted to do all the dumb shit. He is just one of many concerns we have in Goulburn regarding terrorism.'

Pay to Pray

They called them the 'Supermax jihadists', easily recognisable with their beards and beads, shaved heads and Korans, and they forced an unprecedented prison crackdown in 2007 after authorities alleged Islamic extremists were using an al-Qaeda training manual for instruction on how to take over the jail system.

It was alleged that up to 40 inmates in New South Wales had established an internal prison organisation to recruit members to radical Islam and resist interrogation.

Former New South Wales attorney-general John Hatzistergos said extremist leadership groups had been set up across the state's jails. 'The insidious nature of these activities remind us we have to be constantly vigilant to these types of threats for the security of our correctional system.'

Former prison boss Ron Woodham spoke of his conversion fears following the attorney-general's statement. 'There is nothing wrong with conversion to Islam for the right reasons,' he said. 'But we believe there have been conversions taking place for the *wrong* reasons.'

In 2007, 12 of the 37 Supermax inmates were either Muslims or new converts to Islam, and they were described as having a close-knit community inside Australia's most secure jail. And so the monitoring began, including new powers that allowed for the 24-hour surveillance of Muslim inmates in Supermax.

'We have to be able to control every movement and every utterance because of the threat they pose,' Hatzistergos told *Sun Herald* reporter Alex Mitchell. 'We don't want to see any risk to people either inside or outside the system. We simply can't take our eye off them.'

Corrective Services were also suspicious that outside identities and/or groups were transferring money to influence inmates to convert to Islam.

Nightclub murderer and Brothers 4 Life (BFL) founder Bassam Hamzy was singled out as the fundamentalist group's leader and was believed to be responsible for several Islamic conversions. The infamous criminal had a picture of Osama bin Laden seized from his cell.

'We don't have a difficulty with people taking up religion in jail,' Hatzistergos said. 'A lot of people do and that can be beneficial. Where we draw the line is where religion is really a camouflage for other activities. If any person thinks that by taking up religion that somehow it is going to lead to them being treated differently on a day-to-day basis, then they will be sadly mistaken.'

Hamzy, incredibly, may have been using religion as a guise for an audacious escape bid in a prison scam that Woodham described as a 'pay to pray' plot.

'At first [conversions] seemed innocent enough,' said Woodham. 'It wasn't causing any management problems, and we actually gave them prayer mats and things they needed to pray.'

But suddenly they stopped praying.

'That's when we suspected more and began investigating,' Woodham said. 'And over time we realised they were far more organised than we thought.'

Investigations revealed that the inmates who converted were being paid up to $100 a week. The payments were made by way of money orders, originating from Bankstown. They were placed into accounts belonging to associates of the jail converts.

The payments were not just made to inmates at Goulburn, but also to other converts to Islam at prisons across the state. The money was coming from Hamzy's loyal criminal associates on the outside and deposited at his request. Authorities believed Hamzy was buying loyal followers to create a prison gang that would obey his every demand. He would use them to take over the jail and escape in a joint operation conducted with his street gang.

Woodham said Hamzy was the most dangerous inmate in the correctional system.

'This is not the first time he has organised things in jail. He was involved in corrupting staff, who have been charged with corruption. At one stage he was convicted of conspiring to kill a witness against him in a trial using a mobile phone from inside another jail. So he is an extreme high-risk prisoner and a danger, not only in Supermax, but to people on the outside.'

Spy Games

A current guard, who asked not to be named, outlined the new controversial inmate surveillance laws.

'We monitor all their phone calls,' he said. 'All the calls that they make in the yard are monitored, recorded and kept on a database. That system is backed up every week and the file sits there just in case ASIO want anything. Anyone who is deemed flagged, and those flags come down from CIG, their mail is read on the way in and on the way out.'

The following are extracts from the prison case files of the men who have been identified as the Supermax jihadists and/or have been convicted of terror-related offences.

HAMZY, Bassam, DOB: 03/01/1979, received into the HRMCC April 19, 2002
Extreme High Risk Restricted: Classification A1
Hamzy is in Supermax serving a 22-year sentence for the murder of Kris Toumazis outside the Mr Goodbar nightclub in Darlinghurst 1998 and conspiring to murder a key witness while in Lithgow Jail.

'Murder, conspiracy to murder, drug importation, use of a weapon to prevent apprehension, and intel the inmate was heavily involved in illegal and covert activities in jail,' his file reads. 'Drugs, mobile phones and yard disturbances. Alleged to have led an attack on inmate Binse in Unit 3. Involved in corruption of an officer in 2003 in the HRMCC. Involved in passing unauthorised items to his solicitors and misuse of legal phone calls. He is a demanding and covert inmate.

Moved to the STG program at Lithgow, where he ran a substantial criminal empire with mobile phone. Placement at Goulburn MPU July 6, 2008, in segregation.

'Noted as compliant with unit routine,' his file continues, 'but remains a very high-needs inmate. Hamzy is heavily occupied with court matters.'

CHEIKHO, Khaled, DOB: 19/03/1973, received into the HRMCC November 21, 2005
Extreme High Security: Classification AA
One of the 'Terror Five' arrested on charges of purchasing chemicals and explosives with potential targets including the Lucas Heights nuclear reactor in Sydney's south-west.

'Described by sentencing judge as one of the main conspirators in the terrorist offences,' his file reads, 'Cheikho has been noted as compliant with unit routine but has been argumentative with other inmates in the unit. The period of Ramadan has contributed to him being short-tempered.'

CHEIKHO, Moustafa, DOB: 25/02/1977, received into the HRMCC August 3, 2007
Extreme High Security: Classification AA
Another of the men charged in the Sydney terror plot, Moustafa wanted 'violent jihad', which involved the killing of those who did not share his fundamentalist, extreme beliefs.

'AA inmate,' his file reads. 'Nephew of Khaled and seen as a follower that is influenced by his uncle. Cheikho has been noted as being compliant with unit routine. He has been involved in an argument with another inmate in the unit, but this appears to have been settled with staff speaking to him in regards to the problem.'

EL-ASSAAD, Wassim, DOB: 10/11/1977, received into the HRMCC April 14, 2003
Extreme High Security: Classification A2
Sentenced to life for his role in the murder of Kings Cross drug king Danny Karam in December 1998.

'Involved in the White City shoot-out with police,' his file reads. 'Was returned to mainstream population from the HRMCC. Returned to the HRMCC on 27/07/06 after being found in possession of a mobile phone. Involvement in covert activities.'

MAWAS, Rabeeh, DOB: 01/03/1977, received into the HRMCC June 10, 2002
Extreme High Security: Classification A1
Also sentenced to life for the murder of Danny Karam. 'Previous aggressive behaviour towards staff,' his file reads. 'Association with identified security threats. Also involved in contraband. Inmate lost patience and assaulted two staff members in HRMCC. Continues to have little contact with his counsellor, only seeing him for support issues.

*

144

ELOMAR, Mohamed, DOB: 05/03/1965, received into HRMCC November 9, 2005
Extreme High Security: Classification AA
A Terror Five member who plotted a series of attacks in Sydney between July 2004 and November 2005.

'Has extensive financial resources,' his file reads. 'One of the main conspirators, along with Chiekho K. Noted as compliant with unit routine, polite to staff and maintains contact with counsellor for support issues.'

HASAN, Abdul, DOB: 24/08/1969, received into the HRMCC November 21, 2005
Extreme High Security: Classification AA
Another member of the Terror Five, sentenced for his role in planning terror attacks aimed at forcing the Australian government into changing its involvement in both of the Iraq and Afghanistan wars.

'Noted as compliant with unit routine,' his file reads. 'And polite in interaction with staff.'

LODHI, Faheem, DOB: 28/12/1969, received into the HRMCC September 24, 2006
Extreme High Security: Classification AA
A convict arrested for plotting attacks on the national power grid and several Sydney defence installations. He was sentenced in Australia's first major terrorism case, and his incarceration sparked the new AA classification to deal with inmates convicted of terror-related crimes.

'Known recruiter to extreme Islamic views,' his file reads. 'First person to be convicted of terrorist-related offence under the *Anti-Terrorism Act 2005*. Connected to Willie Brigitte in connection with the plot to blow up the Lucas Heights nuclear facility. Noted as compliant with unit routine, polite in his dealings with staff.'

ASLETT, Dudley, DOB: 25/05/1971, received into HRMCC April 2, 2005
Extreme High Security: Classification A1
A Muslim convert in prison for taking part in the brutal 2003 gang rape of a 16-year-old girl.

'Offences of murder and multiple rape attracted signifi-cant media attention,' his file reads. 'Convicted of escape on three occasions, most recently an attempt from court in 1995. He has assaulted two Corrections officers and threatened to kill staff. A lengthy history of self-harm. Has converted to [Islam].

'Aslett appears to be coping well within the unit. He stays out of the politics that occur and has resumed his artwork; this is something that he enjoys and keeps him occupied.'

PRIESTLY, Ronald, DOB: 09/12/1975, received into HRMCC April 17, 2002
Extreme High Security: Classification A1
Another Muslim prison convert sentenced to life for murder. He was also a key figure in the 2002 Goulburn riot.

'Convicted of gaol murder of inmate Lara-Gomez,' his file reads. 'Involved in riot and assaults on officers in Goulburn. Convicted and sentenced to long-term imprisonment for injuries to officers. Most recent threat October 3, 2007 – threatening to kill staff and do what he did to staff [during the riot] on April 16, 2002. He is keen to resume work on literacy course. He is very committed to literacy. Both his sons are incarcerated and he attempts to have contact with them.'

PAULSON, Jamie, DOB: 31/07/1975, received into HRMCC April 17, 2002
Extreme High Security: Classification A1
Paulson was jailed for 22 years for armed robbery and other offences. The Indigenous Australian was converted to Islam while in Goulburn Jail.

'Offences include participate in riot, maliciously inflict GBH [grievous bodily harm], involved in Goulburn riot of 2002,' his file reads. 'Prior convictions of escape. He is compliant with routine and staff directions. He is noted as having minimal interaction with staff. He utilises his associations well in various areas allocated for this purpose. He maintains contact with counsellors and is currently undertaking the "Managing Emotions" program.'

These are just a few of the men secretly and extensively monitored in the prison some officers refer to as the 'Goulburn Super Mosque'.

'But not too many get caught out,' said a current serving Supermax officer. They know their mail is monitored, and it's only the dumb junkies that get caught on the phone. The real threats speak in code.'

Coded Terror

It was revealed in 2014 that convicted terrorists were using a sophisticated code to continue jihadist activities from inside Supermax. Senior Corrections officials came forward with fears that several of Australia's most dangerous inmates were capable of plotting acts of terror because of serious security gaps, even though they were in the most secure level of confinement. The Terror Five are understood to be in shared isolation, with some sharing a cell.

Despite being given the strictest level of inmate classification – the AA classification – these convicts are free to communicate with the outside world through letters, phone calls and visits. Leaked reports also detailed regular visits from family members.

'They are kept in isolation, but that means nothing in jail,' a high-ranking former official said. 'Messages are passed on in many ways. It is not hard because they still get visitation rights, which are their first outlet. They can do it through mail, which they are allowed to send and receive. [The correspondence] is scrutinised and sent to ASIO, but there is still risk. They also receive phone calls.'

The jihadists are effectively operating as a gang inside prison.

A Custody and Sentence Planning report obtained for this book says some AA inmates are recruiting others to terrorism, while some are commanded to attempt escape. Others are ordered to become sleepers and await further instruction. One declassified AA inmate was ostracised by his own terrorist group because he drew too much attention to himself.

'These guys are well prepared before they go to jail,' a former official said. 'They have plans in place for how the cell will operate if they are arrested.' Another former Corrective Services employee said the Terror Five were model prisoners. 'They are very reserved guys,' he said. 'They are all very low key and keep dead quiet. They don't want to jeopardise their cell. They are prepared to sit in prison and make the sacrifice. You will never know what they are thinking.'

Most of the inmates jailed for terror crimes lived in extremely tidy, organised cells and stuck to a strict routine.

Category AA inmates, the report states, 'are those inmates who, in the opinion of the commissioner, represent a special risk to national security (for example, because of a perceived risk that they may engage in, or incite other persons to engage in, terrorist activities) and should at all times be confined in special facilities within a secure physical barrier that includes towers or electronic surveillance equipment'.

Some of the other men held under the AA classification include Mohammed Omar Jamal, who was arrested after authorities found him in possession of bomb-making instructions, 28,000 rounds of ammunition, 12 rifles, militant Islamist literature and footage of beheadings; and Mazen Touma, a suspected member of the Australian Terror

Network found with ammunition and 165 railway detonators after being arrested near the Lucas Heights nuclear reactor.

Khaled Sharrouf became the face of Australian terrorism after a photo of his seven-year-old son holding a severed head shot him to worldwide infamy. He was part of Australia's 2005 terror plot and was jailed after stealing clocks and batteries from Big W. Sharrouf is a chronic schizophrenic and received a disability pension following his release after serving a minimum sentence.

Sharrouf used his brother's passport to escape to Syria last year to fight for the Islamic State. Sharrouf then claimed on Twitter to have received religious instruction while incarcerated from senior al-Qaeda leaders Abu Muhammad al-Maqdisi and Abu Qatada.

'Abu Muhammed almaqdisy use [sic] to give us weekly lessons from the jail phone,' he wrote. 'And we use to get all our knowledge only from those 2.'

He also claimed messages were sent to prisoners through visitors: 'When we needed something answered in prison [we] went through wives.'

A leaked report shows Faheem Lodhi asked for protection from authorities, fearing for his 'personal safety'. He has also been put in 'care under placement' for being a 'threat to good order and discipline'.

Without a Prayer

An intercepted letter from a Caucasian murderer sparked a series of high-level security meetings late in 2014.

'We need to ban all Islamic prayer meetings,' said one of the intelligence officers. 'We have no way of knowing what they are up to. They just can't go on anymore. It's too dangerous.'

The following week at least one prayer session at a Sydney prison was stopped as senior officials considered blanket bans.

The jihadist letter, understood to have been sent by jail convert Leith Marchant, was a convenient excuse for the prayer session to be banned and for calls for further bans to be made, according to a well-placed Corrections official.

'We have had major concerns with prayer meetings for a long time,' the official said. 'They go into a room and we cannot supervise them. We suspect they are talking about more than just God. Letting them meet together and having no idea what's going on is a major security flaw.'

Islamic prayer sessions are held across all New South Wales jails and usually take place on Friday afternoons at 2.30. The inmates are given a room to conduct the weekly meetings; some are attended by an imam. Corrective Services admitted that some prayer sessions had and would continue to be stopped. They also confirmed a de-radicalisation program had been put in place.

'Only specially vetted and accredited imams are allowed to lead the prayers,' a spokesman said. 'The Corrective Services Intelligence Group evaluates all activities on an ongoing basis, and prison management intervenes as required.

'CSNSW has a strict assessment process for when religious leaders seek access to inmates in a correctional centre for religious purposes, under its well-recognised and long-standing chaplaincy program.

'Anyone who applies must undergo strict security and information checks, including having their fingerprints taken and a national criminal record inquiry conducted. Any person who has not resided in Australia for a period of five years or more is also subject to an Interpol check.

'CSNSW is working closely with other intelligence and law enforcement agencies and also provides specialised training to staff to educate on the indicators for radicalised behaviour and how to deal with it.'

The concerns raised by intelligence officers in late 2014 resulted in a drastic linguistic ban that stopped Supermax inmates from talking in Arabic. It was reported by the *Sunday Telegraph* on 8 March 2015 that 13 'Extreme High-Risk Restricted' Goulburn prisoners would be forced to speak strictly in English when communicating with the outside world. New South Wales Attorney-General Brad Hazzard had called for moderate imams to be placed in the state's jails to prevent radicalisation.

'One of the issues that came out of that process was that some of these people, these high-risk inmates, were conducting their discussions in Arabic, or at least not English,' Hazzard said. 'This clearly needed looking at and action, in my view.'

7

CONTRABAND

Backing a Winner

He was a convict no more – papers signed, pre-prison posses-sions returned and an officer escorting him towards the gate.

'I'm going to buy an expensive car,' the fresh freeman said. 'Nothing ridiculous like a Lamborghini or a Ferrari, something more like a Porsche. Maybe even a Beamer or a Merc. That's what I'm going to do first – I'm going to get me some nice wheels. Then I'm going to drive straight to a spray shop and get them to paint a horse on it . . . I'm thinking a charging stallion on the side, you know?'

The officer looked back. He was stumped.

'Why on Earth would you ruin a good car?' he asked. 'Are you kidding me? Wreck the paint job with a *horse*? I can understand why you would want a car, but a car with a *horse* on it?'

'Want me to show you why?' The inmate smirked. 'Hand me your phone.'

Why not? the officer thought. He pulled out his phone, punched in his password and handed it to the done-my-time crook. 'Better be good – I've got a shit data plan.'

Phone now in hand, the former prisoner's grin widened.

'He got on the phone and pulled up the TAB website,' said a current Goulburn officer who asked not to be named. 'He punched in a code and logged into his account.'

The inmate showed the officer the screen.

'His account had a balance of $990,000,' the officer said. 'Almost a million bucks. And he didn't even have a TAB account before he went to Goulburn.'

In fact, this newly minted ex-criminal had never even placed a bet – not before he went to jail and not while in jail. He hadn't studied forms, stewed over odds or screamed winners home . . .

Sure, he'd looked at his TAB account from time to time – he phoned in at least once a week to check his balance – but he never deposited funds or had a punt. He just sat back and listened to how much the balance had grown, the automated voice often making him smile.

'He'd been selling drugs in prison,' the officer said. 'He was well known for it. And he used his betting account to get paid. People would just transfer money into his account to pay for their gear.'

It can be revealed here that the prison drug trade is being funded by sports betting accounts used by inmates to buy and sell anything from Viagra to heroin. Goulburn officers have admitted that the recent proliferation of sports betting companies has made it impossible to stop inmates from using wagering accounts to run a convict drug ring.

'Basically the person you are buying it off will give you a TAB account number and you will get someone on the outside to transfer money into that TAB for you,' said another Goulburn guard.

Inmates in the New South Wales prison system are allowed to make several phone calls a day from a jail landline. They purchase the calls, at a standard rate, with a pre-paid phone card.

'All they have to do then is call the TAB and log into their phone account,' the officer continued. 'From there, they go through the options and into the transfer section. They punch in the account of the guy they are buying it from, and they transfer the amount from their balance into the dealer's account. The dealer will then phone into his account, make sure the money is in, and then he will pass on the drugs.'

A spokesman for Tabcorp Holdings Limited, a government-approved company with 1.2 million regular customers and 310,000 active TAB Sportsbet account holders, who bet through the internet, telephone and pay TV, admitted the transactions would be almost impossible for police and other authorities to trace.

'All they need is an account number and a pin to deposit money into someone else's account,' the spokesman said.

'We wouldn't even be looking at this, and the body that would is a government organisation called AUSTRAC [Australian Transaction Reports and Analysis Centre]. I don't think it would even register for them because they are mainly looking at money laundering and huge sums. They would not be concerned with the amount of money exchanged in single drug deals. Fifty dollars wouldn't register anywhere; you would have to be talking deals in the thousands for it to be looked at.'

News Corp Australia's chief racing writer Ray Thomas said advances in technology and the loosening of legislation has seen a staggering proliferation in the number of betting companies operating in Australia. Inmates can use up to ten different companies to trade cash for drugs, with at least half of the operators based overseas and subject only to limited Australian law.

'Australia was a bit behind other countries when it came to sports betting,' Thomas said. 'But it has gone through the roof in the last decade. The advent of pay TV and the fact you can access so many overseas sports was one of the main reasons for the boom in sports betting. Centrebet, first registered in Alice Springs, Northern Territory, in 1993, was the first company to take sports wagers. The TAB was next in 1998 when they began taking money on rugby league in New South Wales.'

'It is a huge growth industry,' Thomas continued. 'Online betting, and the fact you don't need a retail presence, has brought in huge offshore companies. They operate under different rules, and the TAB really struggled to compete because Australian laws hamstrung them. These overseas operators could put a market on two flies running up a wall. That is slowly changing with legislation freeing up the TAB to compete and open up more markets.'

Thomas said authorities have limited powers when dealing with companies not registered in Australia.

'There are about ten players, but it is difficult to say because a lot of them have recently amalgamated. William Hill [in the UK] sucked up a few of them in one fell swoop. It is changing all the time, but there are only a couple of Australian-based companies. Even Centrebet has been taken over by a company overseas. There would only be about five that are Australian-owned. That would make it very difficult for any type of policing because some of these offshore companies would be very hard to find. They could certainly trace transactions of an Australian-based company, but dealing with the offshore companies would almost be impossible.'

Thomas also said the Australian racing industry has been a long-time target of criminals.

'The racing industry has had some major problems with money laundering. On-track bookies don't have a clue where the money is coming from; they just take the bets. The same with off-course and offshore operators; they will just take the bet. They don't care where the money is coming from. It is an easy way of laundering money.'

Goulburn officers concede they are powerless to stop inmates from using sports betting accounts to buy and sell drugs.

'We are always finding little bits of scrunched-up paper in their cells,' said an officer. 'We open them up and find a bunch of numbers. They are account numbers that the inmate has used to buy drugs. We know what has happened and what the bits of paper mean, but unless we find the drugs, nobody gives a shit.'

The prison officers send the information onto intelligence officers who, in turn, send it to police.

'It wouldn't be high on their list,' said one intelligence officer, 'because it would take a lot of work to get an arrest, and compared to something on the outside it would not be a big bust. We have tried to work with sports betting agencies, but they don't care because it's business. As far as they are concerned, it's legitimate until proven otherwise. Every inmate has a TAB account and they're allowed to have them. I have so many intel holdings on TAB accounts, but they don't amount to shit. I mean, the bloke who walked out with nearly a million dollars? The drugs he sold probably had a street value of 200K, and he may have sold them over ten years. Why would the police try and investigate such a complex network to get a bloke selling 20K's worth of drugs a year? They could pick up a school pot dealer and get the same credit. And the police looking at prisons . . . Well, they are looking at bike gangs and terrorism. All their resources are elsewhere.'

Smuggling

Most contraband in New South Wales is introduced into prisons by way of vagina, claimed a current Goulburn officer. He refers to it as the 'smelly safe'.

'Most of the stuff that comes into prison – drugs, phones, even weapons – comes in by way of a vagina,' said another Goulburn officer who asked to remain anonymous. 'They stick it up their vagina when they come through the screening. We can't see it and the dogs can't smell it. Once they are in they will take it out and put it in their bra before going to the visit. Then they will go to a machine, buy a bag of chips and stick it in with the crisps. She will offer her hubby the chips and he will pull it out and throw it down his overalls. From there he can work it down and push it into his arse. Or the inmate can simply pretend he is eating a chip and swallow it, if [the drug] is in a balloon or well wrapped up. There is no way we can detect it. You would be shocked by the amount of shit that gets in. It's a huge problem, probably the biggest problem we have.'

A can of Coke is also a smuggler's tool of choice.

'The women can just drop a balloon in the can once she has pulled it out of her "safe",' the officer continued. 'Then all she has to do is give her man a sip and he can swallow the druggy bag.'

Contraband has also been smuggled into the jail in lettuce (a mobile was found in a salad on its way into Supermax in 2001); sardine tins (again, a mobile, but this time headed into the Silverwater's Metropolitan Remand and Reception Centre); and, of course, by way of tennis ball, the old Slazenger pegged over prison walls packing drugs, SIM cards and miniature mobile phones.

Here is a list of contraband seized from visitors during a 16-month period, ending in 2009:

- GUNS: loaded and cocked 9mm pistol with 15 rounds; a .22 Ruger rifle and ammunition
- KNIVES: 15, ranging from a flick knife to a 50-centimetre meat clever
- DRUGS: heroin, cannabis, ecstasy, ice, methadone, horse tranquilisers and antidepressants
- CASH: $8465.64
- DRUG PARAPHERNALIA: 150 needles, bongs, 100 deal bags and electronic scales
- ALCOHOL: three Bacardi Breezers, seven West Coast Coolers, a bottle of Bundaberg rum, vodka and a wine
- OTHER CONTRABAND: five pornographic DVDs, curry powder, two fake IDs, body lotion and lip gloss.

Oh, and then there was this find . . .

Snakes on a . . . Pillow

'This is a random cell search,' the officer said to the young prisoner who was serving 15 years for a string of armed robberies and assaults. 'Do you have any contraband in here?'

The young inmate shrugged. 'Nah, none in here, chief – I'm all sweet.'

The officer looked around: bed, TV, a shelf, neatly folded clothes, white property tub.

'Mate, what's in that tub?' the officer asked.

The inmate shrugged again. 'Just me legal stuff. Letters and files, you know?'

The officer nodded. 'So you wouldn't mind opening it for me?'

The inmate shrugged no more, this time jumping to his feet.

'Nah, chief,' he said, now wide awake. 'Like I said – it's legal stuff. You know? It's private.'

Gotcha. What you hiding in here then . . . Drugs? Phones? Let's find out.

'I'm going to have to take a peek,' the officer said. 'I won't read anything or disturb the files if it is what you say.'

The inmate reluctantly moved away, clearing a path to the plastic tub, which was about half a metre wide and 30 centimetres high.

The officer unbuckled the plastic latch on the side and pulled off the lid.

'Jesus!' he shouted, jumping back. His desperate reverse lunge knocked both the inmate and himself to the floor. 'You are fucking kidding me, right.' He was still on the floor but bum-sliding further away from the box.

'He had two brown snakes in his cell,' said a current Goulburn guard of the incident. 'The poor bloke who found it shit himself. It was just a run-of-the-mill property check.'

Now on his feet, but still safely away from the slithering, hissing box, the officer addressed the inmate. 'Mate, they are brown snakes. Venomous, the mostly deadly snakes in Australia – why do you have them?'

'They're me mates,' he said, returning to his trademark shrug. 'My pets. They keep me company. They can't be dangerous. I sleep with them every night.'

The guard shook his head.

'Where did you get them from?' he continued. 'How did you get them into your cell?'

The inmate smiled. 'Found them in the activities yard. At the back of the oval, over the hill. I just slipped 'em up my sleeve and brought them in here. I didn't think it was a big deal. They aren't buggin' anyone.'

The guard shook his head. Then shook it *again*. And *again*. And *again* . . .

'They were only babies, probably only as long as his forearm,' the guard privy to the find recalled. 'He had brought them back to his room and put them in a property tub. He packed it with some grass and gum leaves and was feeding them insects.

'Can you believe the bloke had actually been *sleeping* with them? He'd had them for about three weeks until we found them. They were small, but even as babies they could have killed him. He was in there for 15 years, and he was a pretty dangerous crim, but not as dangerous as those snakes though . . . What an idiot.'

Ice, Ice, Baby

The inmate swung . . . but his shiv slashed nothing but air.

'Yeah – cop that, cunt,' he said.

He slashed again, this time falling over, his face following his fist into floor.

'How do you like that?' he demanded, his victim apparently the concrete ground.

He eyeballed the floor.

'Ready to die? Here it comes.'

He drove the shiv into cement.

*

'There was one case last year in B Wing where six blokes got paid a shitload of ice to put it on somebody,' said a Goulburn officer. 'But the dickheads took the ice before they did the job and completely botched it. We were pissing ourselves when we reviewed it, because they all went in and stabbed nothing but Easter bunnies. They were tripping over themselves and punching walls. You had a bunch of blokes trying to attack a guy that had already gone. It happened in the showers and they got caught, of course; they were still stabbing Santa when we got there. They were too fucked up to carry it through.'

Welcome to the wacky world of ice and inmates . . .

Several officers interviewed for this book claim that ice has become a prison epidemic, with the drug readily available in all New South Wales jails, thanks to a legislation amendment that stops prison officers from properly searching inmates – particularly where the sun don't shine.

'Ice is the big thing at the moment,' said a current Goulburn officer. 'I'm not sure if it's because it gives a good kick or because it's cheap, but in the last 12 months it's coming in such an amount that we can't keep track of it. We are regularly seizing the drug, in up to eight-gram packages. But when you're finding a lot, you know there is a lot more that you're not finding.'

'No, keep your socks on,' the guard yelled at an inmate. 'Take everything off . . . except your socks.'

The inmate slowly slipped off his white overalls, the standard prison-issue jumpsuit he was made to change into before visiting his friend. He then pulled down his undies, kicking them across the floor. He was now naked . . . except for the socks.

'Stop,' said the guard. 'Stand right there . . . legs apart.'

Another officer walked behind the inmate and bent down, his face about a metre away from the other man's anus.

Yuk . . .

'Okay,' the officer issuing orders said. 'Slowly reach down and take off one sock at a time . . .'

The kneeling officer concentrated on nothing but arse. He had to. He had to wait for that split second when the inmate would unclench his anus.

'It sounds disgusting, but that is what we have to do now to find drugs on inmates returning from visits,' an officer who conducts drug searches said. 'We used to be able to do what we had to do to find it, but new laws have stopped us from searching cavities. We can't go sticking fingers in and we can't ask them to spread anything to look in a cavity. You cannot look up their arses – it's that simple. Do-gooders complained and said it was impeding the inmate's privacy. They said it was shameful and humiliating – and maybe it was – but it was also stopping drugs from getting into prison. Now it's just open slather.'

The amended *Crimes (Administration of Sentences) Act 1999* details how an inmate can be searched. Section 46 states, 'In this clause, strip search means a search of a person or of articles in possession of a person that may include; a) requiring the person to remove all of his or her clothes, and; b) an examination of the person's body, but not of a person's body cavities, and of clothes.'

'That effectively means we can't even ask an inmate to open his mouth,' the guard continued. 'If he was smart and he had drugs in his mouth, he could just refuse. Under the law there would be nothing we could do about it. The commissioner says he will change the legislation, but he hasn't done anything yet. We are not even allowed to look under arms, because that's technically a cavity. The only thing we can do is put them in an observation cell if they refuse. So instead of saying "spread it" and having the stuff just fall out, we are made to go through all this instead. It's beyond a joke.'

But back to the socks . . .

'That's a trick we use to get around it,' the officer said. 'We may have seen something on a camera and we believe the crim has put something up his arse. When everything is off we lift their tackle and tell them to take one sock off at a time. When they bend over to take the sock off you get more of a spread in the arse.

'If you see a bit of plastic or whatever, you give the thumbs up to the boss, and then we use a section of the law where we can use force to seize a dangerous article. We tell them to take it out. If they don't, then we make it very uncomfortable for them. We will basically upend them and hold them there until they remove it. But using that legislation really puts us under the pump because we've used force on an inmate, which is a big thing. It all has to be documented and we come under scrutiny. They are taken to the medical staff to make sure they have no injuries, and it leaves us open to being charged.'

But, even with the sock-reaching and use-of-force loophole, drugs get in.

'[Inmates] go in with overalls that are tight around the wrists and ankles to try and stop them from putting anything up their sleeves,' the guard said. 'But they still manage to get it in and work it into their arses. Even with the ability to look in cavities, stuff still gets in. One of the reasons is just human error. In that strip-search section there are only two blokes that will search 60 guys coming in, and then search the same 60 going out. The last half of the searches aren't going to be as good as the first half – that's just human nature.'

'Alcohol used to be a huge problem,' the guard added, 'but we don't have that anymore. We used to always find bags of fermenting brew and come across drunk prisoners. But we don't anymore because, instead of waiting five or six days for a brew to ferment and risk having it found, they can get a hit of ice; just walk into the cell next door and buy a hit. It is cheap and it is everywhere.'

Inmates affected by ice can be extremely difficult to deal with, according to the officer.

'Ice can give some men the strength of 20 bulls,' he said. 'And the confidence to take on an army. We have big problems getting some of them down but, in saying that, the drug also zonks others. It affects them all differently. I think an aggressive person will become more aggressive on ice and vice versa. But most people in jail are aggressive by nature.

'They also become very confident. If you tell them to stop doing something they do not listen. This has all been iden-tified on daily intelligence briefs and is spoken about on a daily basis. Searching for ice is one of the biggest priorities in the prison; unfortunately we are just very reactive at the moment.'

Tiny Tablets

Even harder to find, and possibly more problematic than ice, is a prescription drug called buprenorphine. Used to treat opioid dependence on the outside, the tiny little tablet has created a crisis on the inside.

'Buprenorphine comes in a wafer that is about a quarter of the size of a fingernail,' said a Goulburn officer. 'It's so small that they can hide it their ears, between their fingers, in their belly buttons. It's impossible to detect.'

Prison officials in America have admitted they are powerless to stop the drug entering their jails. It can be crushed into a paste and spread over stamps, sewn into shoes and put into the spines of magazines.

It is also readily available and can be obtained legally and bought for a dollar a hit.

'It's a pharmaceutical drug prescribed for heroin addicts,' the guard continued. 'It is used in the same way as methadone; it just has a much bigger bang. People on the outside can easily get a script for the drug and, instead of taking it, they can sell it to prisoners and make a massive profit. One wafer outside is worth a dollar, and one inside is worth a $100. They divide them up in quarters, which they call a "spot", and they sell them for $25 each. It is an unstoppable trade. Everyone is taking it, and we can't do anything about it.'

Jan Shuard, Commissioner for Corrections Victoria, spoke to the ABC about the drug in Victorian jails.

'In the last 12 months we conducted 84,600 searches in our prisons,' she said. 'We did 7000 random, general urine tests. What is most concerning is 60 per cent of those tests were positive to buprenorphine. We have found strips of bup under a stamp on a letter and hidden within a matchbook, so there's a range of ways that it can be brought in.'

Prawns and Paper

He slowly pulled the package from the bin.

Is it drugs? Is it a bomb?

'Whatever it was it had been wrapped neatly, with a lot of care,' said former officer Ian Norris. 'We were doing a sweep through that area on one particular night, and I happened to look in a garbage bin. There was a parcel in there that didn't look quite right. It wasn't just crumpled up newspaper or something like that. It was a newspaper parcel that had been wrapped neatly and tied up with a piece of cloth.'

Norris was on B watch on a cool, clear night in 1996. He and a fellow officer were patrolling the outer perimeter. Like always, they paid particular attention to the historic St Saviour's Cemetery, just beyond the prison walls to the south.

'We would have a bit of a search around the jail because we would get all types hanging around,' Norris said. 'In the cemetery at the back, it was quite usual practice for the drug dealers to hide things. One of the places they kept things was in the rubbish bins, but they would also hide them under the gravestones, places like that.'

That's right. The dead don't talk – so why not use them to help smuggle drugs into the jail? Even Captain William Hovell, the great Australian explorer who was buried in St Saviour's in 1824, was an unknowing accomplice.

'The cemetery is right behind main jail, the MPU, which was supposed to be the jail to end all jails and escape-proof,' Norris said. 'The minimum-security blokes used to go over there for charitable purposes, mow the lawn and generally tidy it up. They kept the cemetery in reasonable nick, and it gave them an opportunity to smuggle drugs. Dealers would come along and hide the drugs in little rabbit holes near the graves. They might dig a little hole directly under a tombstone and stick their stash there.'

The gravestones were foolproof markers for the drug dealers.

'They would give the crims a name over the phone,' Norris said. 'The name of a dead bloke. The crims would then just find the tombstone, pick up the stash, put it in their pocket and walk it back into jail. Plenty of drugs were found in that cemetery, and that's why we were checking it that night.'

Norris poked at the package with a torch.

'I thought it was too big to be drugs,' Norris said. 'And it didn't go "boom" when I poked it, so I didn't think it was a bomb. But we thought we should report it and hand in the package, as that was prison protocol.'

The shift supervisor looked at the package and said, 'It's a bloody bomb. Get that friggin' thing out of here. Quick, run it back to the bin. Put it back in there before you get us all killed.'

So Norris ran a delicate egg-and-spoon race back to the bin.

Meanwhile, the night senior was calling the bomb squad a few hours away in Sydney. They packed their equipment into their blast-proof van and hit the road.

'They didn't arrive until 3 o'clock in the morning,' Norris said. 'They unloaded all their gear and went in to expect.'

Soon the bomb disposal robot was armed, showing its muscle by firing a shot into the bin.

Boom.

'It rained prawns,' Norris said. 'There was no bomb in the package, of course, and that is what I'd told the night senior when he suggested it was a bomb. The blast from the robot ripped the bin to pieces and sent prawn shells flying. God knows why anybody would do it, but someone had neatly wrapped up all these prawn shells and an empty can of Coke, and thrown the package in the bin.'

Needless to say the bomb boys were not impressed. Neither was the Department of Corrective Services when they were given the bill for blasting the bin.

'The night senior basically dumped all the blame on us,' Norris said. 'Nothing was mentioned about the officer in the gate claiming it was a bomb. Nothing was mentioned about the night senior telling us to take it back. The whole thing was so bloody hilarious that it was stupid. It was quite an embarrassment to the jail and obviously a waste of valuable resources. I copped the blame for it, despite not doing a thing wrong.

'Some good did come out of it, though. That bin was a notorious spot for hiding drugs. They shot it to shit and it was never replaced.'

Dildos

'Ah,' said the senior guard. 'What do we have here?'

He held the suspected contraband in his hand, rubbing it up and down as he looked into the eyes of the inmate.

'Don't touch that, chief,' the prisoner began to beg. 'Please don't touch that. Not that.'

The officer cracked the shits.

'What?' he yelled, gripping the contraband more tightly. 'I'll touch whatever I damn well want to touch.'

The inmate asked again, softer this time, a slight smirk on his face.

'Chief,' he said, 'put it down. You don't want to be touching that.'

'And why not?' the officer screamed, really angry now. 'Why do you think you can tell me what I should and shouldn't be touching?'

The inmate frowned, smile gone.

'Because it's my dildo, chief,' he said. 'And I just had it up my arse.'

The officer dropped the hard, moist object. Then he turned a bright shade of red.

It's not just drugs that are seized from cells. There are other types of contraband, not always lethal but certainly disgusting.

Smelly Safe

Shoulders back, eyes forward, she slowly edged her way to the front of the queue.

Alyce Jay Bell knew the routine. First the guard would ask her if she was concealing anything on or in her body. She would say no. Then he would give her a rushed feel – overworked hands quickly brushing at legs and stomach before lightly touching shoulders and arms. They would find nothing.

And then she would be shown to a table where her husband would be sitting and smiling, of course, because seeing her was the highlight of his long, lonesome week.

Just a typical Sunday, really.

Tap. Tap.

'Excuse me, miss,' said the guard. 'Could you please come with me?'

Alyce was stunned, her Sunday routine ruined.

'Me?' she asked. 'What? Where? Why?'

The guard was not mucking around.

'We have reason to believe you may be attempting to bring contraband into the prison,' he said. 'Please come this way.'

Oh no.

Her shoulders slumped and her eyes hit the ground.

'Mmm,' she said. 'Okay.'

Alyce had been spotted by a guard having a quick fiddle, her hands going down to her crotch for a back and forth. The eagle-eyed officer – apparently neither rushed nor over-worked that day – suspected more than an innocent scratch.

'We have detained you because we believe you are trying to bring contraband into the jail,' the officer said. 'We are now giving you an opportunity to hand over the item, or items, that we believe you have attempted to hide on your body.'

Alyce stuck her hand down her pants. *Better give them a little or they will find a lot.*

She pulled out three balloons filled with white powder, before carefully placing them on a countertop.

'Is that all?' the officer asked. 'Do you have anything else on or in your body?'

Haven't I given them enough?

'No,' she said. 'That's it.'

The officer thought she was lying – he was *sure* she was lying.

'Miss, we suspect you are carrying more items on or within your body,' the guard continued. 'We will be required to take you to Goulburn Police Station for the purpose of a full-body examination unless you remove the items now.'

She fluttered her eyes.

'And then will you let me go home?' she asked. 'I just want to go home.'

'No,' the guard replied. 'But compliance will be looked upon favourably.'

She decided to take her chances.

Alyce Jay Bell was arrested and taken to Goulburn Police Station, where she produced a condom containing two mobile phones, two micro SIM cards and two USB charging cables. Police alleged she had secreted the items in her vagina. Bell was charged and convicted of attempting to deliver things to an inmate without lawful authority, possessing a restricted substance and attempting to bring a small quantity of drugs into a place of detention. The powder she volunteered to the Corrections staff was later revealed to be steroids.

Online Shopping
2.2 TOUCH SCREEN, ANDROID SMART PHONE. Only 81mm x 45mm and just 11mm thick. No bigger than a cigarette lighter.

The eBay seller goes on to list some of the phone's features.

32GB, Micro USB, 512 RAM, hands-free loudspeaker, text and calls, email, web, GRRS, stream video and WI-FI.

And all this for the inmate-friendly price of $119.90, with free delivery.

'Mobile phones are everywhere in jail,' said an officer who asked to remain anonymous. 'You can get these BMW branded mobile phones, and they are tiny. In the last six months we've found about two dozen. Some of those are through cell searches and some are pulled up coming through visits: [the inmates] shove them up their arses.

'These Bluetooth phones they make are smaller than a box of matches. The yards and cells are searched, but the main way we get them is through intelligence. We do random searches, of course, but low staffing levels are putting a limit on how many we can do. I couldn't even take a guess at how many [phones] are in the prison right now.'

Online traders, mostly based in China, are directly marketing miniature phones to inmates. The following selling point was pulled off an advertisement for a phone that was designed to look like the electronic key fobs used to transmit signals to unlock cars: 'Very, very low metal content badge, which can be removed due to metal content alarm.'

Selling for under $100, the 'FOB Key Phone' won't set off a metal detector, and it can also be used to send text messages. They come branded with car manufacturers' logos – BMW, VW and Porsche are among the most popular.

Brothers 4 Life gang general Mohammed Hamzy is facing charges after a BMW key fob was found in his Silverwater jail cell in July 2014. According to the police statement, a charging device was also found within the wall.

Hamzy told the officers, 'It's BMW. It's mine.'

The find forced current Corrective Services boss Peter Severin to admit that mobile phones were a major problem in New South Wales prisons: 'Contraband mobile phones, including mini key ring phones, are an issue for correctional jurisdictions around the world. New South Wales is no different.'

There are also phone watches available from $79, but among inmates the popular choice seems to be the fob phones. A staggering 7000 of them have been seized from jails in the United Kingdom, and the government is attempting to ban their sale. In New South Wales prisons alone, 92 mobile phones were seized within a 21-month period leading up to 2001.

The phones enter prison in a number of ways: visitors can bring them in by way of body cavity, corrupt officers can sell them to crooks, and they can even be thrown over walls.

'Prisoners are increasingly using ingenious ways to sneak in and hide mobile phones,' said former Corrective Services minister Richard Amery. 'We all know they are getting smaller and therefore increasingly hard to detect. Mobiles are a valuable commodity in prisons and can be used to organise criminal activities outside of jail.'

Even murder . . .

Murder by Mobile

Bassam Hamzy stood and smiled, not one bit bothered by the handcuffs, the bright orange jumpsuit or his new home – a 6-metre by 3-metre cell in Goulburn's Supermax. He had just been moved from Lithgow Correctional Centre to Australia's most secure jail after being caught with a mobile phone, which he was suspected of using to run a $1.5 million drug empire. And now he was about to be charged with 15 offences he allegedly committed with the aid of a phone while behind bars.

But still he smiled, even as police dragged him away.

The mobile phone would soon be exposed as prison's most dangerous weapon . . .

Bassam Hamzy took the mobile into the prison toilet.

'Can you slap him once in the face?' he ordered, quietly but forcefully.

'I've already done it, cuz,' came the reply from his Brothers 4 Life foot soldier. 'I've already chopped him . . . I've got blood everywhere, man.'

Speaking on a different day, but with the same phone, Hamzy reinforced his demands: 'Let me speak to him before you cut his ears off so he can hear what I'm saying. If I ever have to come up there again, I'm gunna cut all his fingers off . . . Next time I'll take his ears and make them into a necklace.'

These were just two of the threats, orders and ultimatums Hamzy issued over his mobile phone in 2008, when he made a staggering 19,523 calls in just six weeks. Yep . . . a maximum-security prisoner in Lithgow Jail making 250 calls a day from the slammer.

The founder of the notoriously violent gang led by his cousin Mohammed, Bassam Hamzy ordered hits, demanded kidnappings and arranged drug deals. After it was revealed that police had been listening to the phone calls Bassam had placed from May to June 2008, he pleaded guilty to all 15 charges, including supplying a commercial quantity of meth-amphetamine from his cell and orchestrating the kidnapping of John Baroutas in Adelaide on 5 June 2008.

He also admitted to supplying 600 grams of 3, 4-MDMA (ecstasy) and 15.75 kilograms of cannabis; using a false or stolen American Express card to book two Qantas airfares; ordering a house in Melbourne to be 'sprayed' with bullets because of a $45,000 drug debt; and setting up his own ABN for drug transactions.

A document tendered in court during his trial drove home the reach of Hamzy's criminal empire: 'Bassam Hamzy obtained a mobile phone and made a number of phone calls, organising the sourcing of various prohibited drugs in Sydney and their direction to Melbourne, where they were supplied to associates for on-supply.'

He was sentenced to an additional 14 years for these contraband crimes.

'It just shows you how serious the problem is,' said a current Goulburn guard.

'Some people might think, *What's the big deal?* They think they are just calling their girlfriends or mums. Well, that may be the case for most of them, but some of them are also killing people with their phones and dealing drugs. They are doing exactly the things that being locked up was supposed to stop.'

Part of Hamzy's punishment was being made a resident of Goulburn's Supermax. With a combined minimum sentence of 36 years, Hamzy was slapped with an A1 prisoner classification – the highest security rating possible – and put in a solitary cell.

'He has had a bunch of restrictions put on him,' the guard continued. 'He isn't allowed to speak Arabic on the phone, he is mostly kept in solitary, and all of his conversations are recorded and his mail is read.'

Still, Hamzy could not be silenced.

It was revealed in 2013 that Hamzy had been 'communicating' with the outside world through a woman posing as his lawyer. Authorities alleged the gang leader was using privileged legal visits to bypass his strict security conditions to send orders to his street gang.

Mobile phones are used for much more than making telephone calls from behind bars. Aside from accessing the internet and web-based applications, inmates can also receive information from the outside world by way of Secure Digital (SD) cards.

'It is very easy to smuggle an SD card into jail,' said a Goulburn officer. 'They are tiny and almost impossible to pick up in a search. They can also be sent in through the mail and are not detected by scanners. The inmate can then load them into his phone and extract whatever information has been put on it.'

And most of that is porn.

'There is a lot of porn on the cards we find,' the officer continued. 'They don't have to bother with magazines because these cards are much easier to get in, and instead of just pictures they are getting full-on videos. There was a smart phone found in the Islander Yard this year [2015] with some really hardcore stuff on it. That's pretty common these days.'

And phones can also be walked straight in with a guard . . .

Capturing Cale

14 March 2003. Armed with a screwdriver, a video camera and an empty evidence bag, the two officers entered the cell. They had received information that the inmate known as 'C2' was keeping a mobile phone in his HRMU cell. Supermax has the most sophisticated prison security system in Australia: X-ray machines, metal detectors, surveillance cameras and a prisoner-to-guard ratio as high as four to one. No one can get out and nothing can get in.

Well . . . that's what they had hoped.

Camera rolling, evidence bag open and ready, they checked the bed. *Nothing.* They checked the shelves. *Nothing.* They checked the toilet. *Nothing.*

All clear.

And then out came the screwdriver and out came the screws. The cover plate of the cell's wall light unit was removed and *behold*: two mobile phones and four SIM cards. Incredible. The inmate was running his criminal empire from a Supermax cell.

But the guards were not done yet. They placed the phones and the SIM cards in the evidence bag and moved their search next door to the cell of another inmate, known as 'C1'.

They checked the bed. *Nothing.* They checked the shelves. *Nothing.* They checked the toilet. *Nothing.*

All clear.

Out came the screwdriver, off came the cover plate, and *behold*: two more phones, two more SIM cards, a mobile phone charger, a miniature digital camera and a ratchet that could be used to remove the light unit.

The once-empty evidence bag now full, the officers reported their find. And so the investigation began – warrants were obtained and listening devices planted.

Correctional officer Cale David Urosevic walked over to the boom gate. He began talking to a man called 'Lou'. He didn't know they were watching. He didn't know they were listening.

'Did I miss any of your phone calls?' Lou asked.

'No,' the officer replied.

'Oh, okay,' Lou said. 'I just missed . . . I had a few phone numbers, and I didn't know whose they bloody were, and I thought, *Oh fuck, maybe I'm missing them and –*'

'No,' the officer interrupted. 'Not while he's down there. It's just too . . . too in the focus at the moment.'

'Yeah right,' Lou said, nodding. 'With all those other dramas you were telling me about? All of those dramas with them getting caught out and stuff?'

'Well, that's it,' said the officer. 'Yeah, they are searching. They're bringing in all these new things into place so we can't take anything down there at all. So at the moment, I can't see it happening with him.'

Lou nodded again. 'Oh, okay. So where has he been moved now? Is he still in Supermax?'

'It's where he was when he first got caught,' said the officer.

'Oh, okay.' Lou looked puzzled. 'Oh, right – and you don't even want to risk taking it down there?'

Corrections officer Urosevic then started talking of 'organics'.

'Maybe just the organics,' he said, 'if you still wanted that, but nothing electrical – that's the thing, see? – because that will get caught and there will be a big frenzy over it if there's something else found down there.'

Lou smiled. 'I've got ten steroid tablets he wants.'

'Only ten?' the officer asked. 'He wants about 300 of the fuckers.'

'I know,' Lou replied, 'but I have a few cards and a few pay cards as well, but if you don't want to take them in I understand.'

Officer Urosevic then spoke to Lou about the new security measures.

'It's just a matter of time,' he said. 'Because I am not down there as often as I was before.'

'Well, all right,' Lou said. 'All I've got is ten and I've got, you know, I've got money and that, if you want money and all that sort of stuff?'

The officer paused for a moment. 'Yeah, how about the Maccas on the way out of town? I should be there about ten past four or so.'

Lou was pleased. 'Well, you work out how much you want, bro,' he said. 'It was two thousand bucks last time, wasn't it?'

Officer Urosevic shook his head. 'It was four.'

'But that was with the phones and that as well. But ten doesn't sound like enough tablets for him?'

Lou left the officer and walked into the prison, where he visited the inmate known as C1.

He then picked up his conversation with Urosevic (as do the police's listening devices) when he finished his visit.

'How'd you go?' the officer asked.

'Yeah, so a total of five,' Lou replied. 'That's what he has asked for because it was better that way. You don't have to hold so many.'

The officer looked nervous. 'Yeah, well, I was thinking about that. It's still the same level, whether it's one trip for a small amount or a big amount.'

'Yeah, mate, no worries.' Lou said. 'So four?'

'Yep.' The officer nodded.

'Well, I've got it,' Lou said, ending the conversation. 'I'll see you at Maccas at a quarter past.'

And sure enough he did. Lou jumped into the passenger seat of Urosevic's car.

'Count it if you want,' Lou said, 'but it's all there – four large ones.'

The officer shrugged his shoulders and flicked through the wad of cash he had just been handed. 'Yeah, looks about right.'

He then took the pills and shook Lou's hand. Deal done, he plucked a gear and pulled onto the highway.

Wheee-yooor! Wheee-yooor! Wheee-yooor!

The police siren filled his ears as the red and blue flashing lights filled his rear-view mirror.

Gotcha!

Urosevic's car was intercepted by NSW Police and officers of the Independent Commission Against Corruption (ICAC).

They searched his car, finding $4,000 and ten tablets, later identified as steroids.

The disgraced officer was caught red-handed and was forced to admit to his crimes, detailing how, in addition to the drugs, he had smuggled mobile phones into Australia's most secure jail: he'd simply walked them in on his person.

'I walked in through the metal detector,' he said. 'And it went off as it always does for everybody that goes through, and then I lined up for parade duty.'

Despite setting off the alarm, the officer was never searched.

Urosevic was dismissed on 13 August 2003. He pleaded not guilty to a string of criminal charges, claiming he had acted under duress after threats were made against him and his family. Urosevic was sentenced to 500 hours of community service.

Can't Find 'Em? Block 'Em.

There is only one solution to stopping inmates from committing contraband crimes in prison: make the mobile phones useless.

Authorities here and in other countries, like the UK and the US, have admitted that many factors – the ever-decreasing size of mobile phones, mercenaries who will market phones exclusively to inmates, the ceaseless ingenuity of prisoners – make it mission impossible to prevent convicts from getting their hands on the potentially deadly devices.

And they also agree that the only solution to fixing the problem is by using technology to block mobile phone signals in and around the prison.

'We believe jamming technology is the ultimate answer,' said Corrective Services commissioner Peter Severin, 'because even if an inmate does obtain a mobile phone, it will be worthless.'

The installation of dozens of these antennas, which emit a very low-powered blocking signal, make it impossible for anyone in the jail to receive their own mobile signal, preventing the inmate from making calls, receiving text messages and using the internet and web-based applications. Prisoners can still use other functions on the phone, like video recorders and players, to view information that may be smuggled in on SD cards.

In 2013 Corrective Services, along with the New South Wales government, announced that a nine-month trial of this jamming technology, which has been successfully introduced overseas, would go ahead at Lithgow Jail, where 239 mobile phones had been seized from inmates that year.

There were a few obstacles: the trial had to be approved by the Australian Communications and Media Authority since it is an offence to operate, possess or supply jamming equipment. And it would cost an estimated $1.06 million.

Minister for Justice Greg Smith endorsed the Australian-first trial that would run in Lithgow Jail beginning September 2013, saying, 'Mobile phones pose a threat to the security of correctional centres and community safety, as they are often used to facilitate crime outside prison walls.'

The trial was extended by an extra three months, and the year-long Lithgow experiment finished in late 2014. Corrective Services have prepared a report to be examined by the Australian Communications and Media Authority. The use of this technology to stop this serious problem seems to be a no-brainer, but there are concerns to quell and hurdles to jump.

A full rollout of the technology across Australian prisons will need approval from the major telecommunications companies like Telstra, Optus and Vodafone. There are concerns that the antennas may block mobile phone signals not only in the jail but in areas close by.

Officers are crossing their fingers.

'The only solution to this problem is phone blocking,' said one Goulburn warder. 'They have to do it, and I am sure they will do it. But it could be a while. They don't quite have the technology right at the moment to narrow the area it will affect. There are houses right near Goulburn Jail, and there are genuine concerns that their phone reception will be affected. There were a few issues with the Lithgow trial, but hopefully those issues will be resolved because this will fix a very serious problem.'

The Department of Corrective Services was reluctant to speak about the trial when approached for this book.

And maybe this is why . . .

'The technology does not work,' said another officer. 'We seized over 30 phones from Lithgow during the jamming period. They are still smuggling them in and they are still using them because they can still make calls. They have walked around the jail with their phones and worked out where they can get a signal and where they can't get a signal. Some of them get signals right at the back of their cells, and they all get a signal out in the yard at the back of the basketball court. It has all been kept hush-hush because the department has spent a lot of money on it and it doesn't work. The problem can't be solved with the technology they have trialled. It's like most things ... The inmates eventually find a way around it because they have nothing but time on their hands to find a way to beat whatever is put in place.'

The Stone Age

Before mobiles, the Jurassic landline was the major problem in prisons. An escape at Goulburn Jail in 1996 was believed to have been organised, in part, by the use of a landline available to prisoners. Others had ordered hits and intimidated witnesses on the phone. In the wake of the escape by notorious drug dealer George Savvas, the New South Wales government introduced a new telephone system to prevent 'call crime'.

Called the 'Controlled Telephone System', inmates were only allowed to phone six preselected numbers. Calls were monitored by security staff and limited to six minutes; a pre-recorded message alerted the receiving party where the call was originating from, along with the caller's identity.

'This is a big improvement on the old system,' said former Corrective Services minister Bob Debus. 'Before, inmates could make calls to unlimited numbers from normal public pay phones, with the only control the random possibility of their calls being monitored. The inmates were given a pin number and charged 40 cents for the call: the amount withdrawn from a phone card. But all that is useless when you have the internet . . .'

Status Busted

The inmate checked his hair. *Sweet.* And then the light. *Sweet.*

He turned to face the camera and framed his shot.

Prison greens? *Check.* Cell bars? *Check.* Handsome inmate? *Check.*

He pressed his thumb against the screen.

Click.

Jesse Sbrugnera, a small-time crook, smiled at his selfie – the first to ever be taken in prison.

Yeah, sweet, he thought.

But Sbrugnera wasn't finished. He wanted to create more history by becoming the first inmate to ever update his social media status from inside prison walls.

Knock. Knock.

'Cell search,' the guard yelled. 'We're coming in.'

Sbrugnera was no longer smiling. *Maybe posting that picture wasn't such a good idea after all?*

'We have reason to believe you are hiding contraband,' the guard said. 'We believe you have a smart phone somewhere in this cell.'

Yep. Not a good idea at all.

Sbrugnera is not what you would call a criminal master-mind. He was first sentenced to four years in jail for robbery. On 25 February 2009, he'd stolen $300 from a girl opening the Subway fast food restaurant in Lee Wharf, Newcastle, before going to a nearby Aldi supermarket and taking $100 from a cashier, punching him in the face afterwards. He then went to a pub, where he was found shoving the cash into a poker machine.

'We went in the day after the [selfie] post,' recalled an officer. 'We turned his cell upside down, and of course we found the phone. Intelligence officers picked up his photo almost as soon as it was uploaded. To think you could take a picture of yourself from within your cell and then post it from within your cell and not get busted is absolutely stupid.'

8

ESCAPE

Malibu and Pineapple

Is she looking at me? thought the off-duty guard, schooner in one hand, TAB ticket in the other. *Nup. I couldn't be that lucky.*

He took a swig of his sixth beer, more half-empty than half-full, before clunking the glass down on the cardboard coaster.

It was Saturday night and the Goulburn Soldiers Club was unusually busy. A band had the auditorium bobbing, old rock-and-roll covers fuelling the dancing and drinking. A couple of ladies – late 40s, maybe early 50s – twisted and turned on the parquetry floor. They smiled at the drunk boy hoping to land himself a cougar. He swaggered and swayed on the edge of the dance floor, oblivious to the pack of cougar husbands that would soon offer to show him outside.

Six or seven men showboated at the bar while they waited to order drinks. The leggy blonde standing at the front of the line had them puffing out chests and sucking in guts. She ordered a Malibu and pineapple, grabbed a straw and left the beer line posse.

'Whoa,' one said. 'You don't get that in here every day.'

Back at the table, now on his seventh schooner, TAB ticket torn in half, the off-duty guard looked for the blonde he'd seen at the bar.

Then he saw her; she was walking his way.

Maybe this is my lucky night.

He performed a minor magic trick, making his wedding ring disappear from his finger.

'Excuse me,' she said. 'Is this seat taken?'

The guard acted surprised. 'Oh, no. Take it. I'm on my own.'

The blonde smiled. 'Sorry, I don't want to take it.' She grinned. 'I was wondering if I could join you. I'm here from Sydney on my own, and I was hoping for some company.'

She extended her hand and gave him a name – a false one. No one would ever know her real name. She would simply be known as the mystery blonde who created the chaos that allowed a maximum-security prisoner to simply walk out of Goulburn Jail.

Toilets and Tantrums
6 July 1996

Andrew Georgious Savvas, serving 30 years for conspiring to import $200 million worth of heroin, walked into the 'sterile area', a foyer-like room on the edge of the industries building. Old metal detectors designed to discover chisels and hammers littered the area. Next door was the spray shop, which was now serving as the visits centre because of upgrades to other parts of the prison.

George, as he was known, was particularly jovial on this day.

'Afternoon, boys,' he said. 'Maybe it's a good sort that's come to visit me. Can you cut a hole in the crotch so I can get the big fella out?'

The guards were not amused and ordered the inmate to strip. They took his prison greens and issued him with a white, pocketless jumpsuit with full-length sleeves and legs.

'Put them on and turn around,' the officer fired.

Now wearing only undies and socks, Savvas slipped on the jumpsuit after a body search.

'How am I supposed to cop a blowjob in this?' Savvas asked.

The guard took a cable tie from the table and threaded it through the first of two metal eyeholes located on the back of the jumpsuit. Tight at the wrists, ankles and neck, the suit was a security measure put in place to prevent inmates from slipping contraband into their suits then into a body cavity.

'You'll just have to wait until tonight,' the guard said. 'I'm sure your boyfriend will give you a reach-around.'

Savvas sauntered into the spray shop at about 12.30pm, all smile and swag. He went over to an empty table, pulled out a chair and sat down. He had his choice of tables, but chose to sit directly under the viewing room – a glass box containing a guard charged with monitoring the area. He looked up and couldn't see the guard. Good. That meant the guard couldn't see him either.

Savvas, a former sports entrepreneur, hotelier, developer and Marrickville alderman, among other things, sat back in his chair as the other 89 inmates continued to flood in and find tables. He looked around; there were six guards in the room. They were watching the inmates, who were all beaming as they waited to see loved ones.

At 1pm, two men walked into the room. They had shown ID and had been searched before signing in for an official visit. Savvas showed little emotion when they approached him, greeting them with only a limp handshake. Watched by a security camera directly above, Savvas conversed with the two men who were visiting him for the first time. The room was now buzzing with inmates finding out about tries scored by sons, daughters getting married, brothers fighting at the pub. They laughed, hugged and smiled in this rarest of moments that made them feel free.

'Chief,' Savvas yelled. 'Chief, over here. I need to go to the toilet.'

The guard walked over. It was 1.40pm.

'Righto, let's go,' the officer said, escorting Savvas to the toilet, as per procedure, and returning him to his two visitors when he was done.

And that's when all hell broke loose . . .

A chair toppled over and slapped the concrete floor as the prisoner shot to his feet.

'You're nothing but a slut,' he screamed at the visiting woman. 'Guard. GUARD! Get me out of here now. I want to go back and watch the fucking football.'

A guard rushed in. 'You two break it up,' he demanded. 'And you . . . come with me. You're going back.'

Six guards became five.

Another chair upended.

'It's over!' a woman yelled at an inmate. 'I'm getting a divorce. And by the way, I've been rooting Joe.'

Five guards became four.

'Officer,' another woman approached the guard, 'I need to go to the toilet. You need to escort me, don't you?'

Four became three.

Starting to get the picture?

'It was just chaos,' former prison officer Ian Norris recalled. 'There were domestics, people asking to be taken out, people getting up left, right and centre. Nothing like that had ever happened before. All these blues going off at the same time.'

But the fighting wasn't over. The visitors pushed and shoved, desperate to get out.

'It had $1500 in it,' a woman screamed at the officer guarding the exit. 'Someone stole my purse out of the locker. Was it you? *Was it you, big man?* Do you have a key?'

The visitors were whisked out and the prisoners returned to their cells. The visits room was now quiet, now empty – well, except for chairs, tables and a shredded white jumpsuit.

The alarm was raised. It was 2.37pm.

Ian Norris was working in 2 Tower when the siren started to wail.

'It was pandemonium,' he said. 'We didn't know who had escaped or how they'd escaped – we just knew *someone* had escaped. They'd found a pair of overalls stashed under a table.'

The jail was shut down and the inmates were all sent to muster. One by one, their names were marked off and their cell doors slammed shut. But one cell remained open. One name unchecked on the list: Andrew Georgious Savvas.

'We couldn't believe he was gone,' said Norris. 'How could a crim walk out with visitors? There was a guard sitting in the old office watching down. There were another six in the room. And then there were the cameras. The cameras were watching everything, and that's how we found out what had happened.'

'An escape!' Governor Allan Chisholm screamed. 'Through visits . . . You have to be fucking kidding me. You mean to tell me a maximum-security inmate just walked out onto the street?'

Chisholm, now retired and living on a property in rural Queensland, has broken his 18-year silence to set the record straight about the escape that would ruin his career, the finger unfairly pointed at him.

'The first thing we did was look at the videos,' Chisholm recalled. 'That's how we found out how he got out. You have to remember that this thing didn't happen in the normal visiting section. It was being held down in the industrial complex because renovations were taking place. I don't think it could have happened had it not been for the construction.

'Anyway, we went through the video. It was all pretty normal until a domestic blue broke out. There was one at first, and then another, and soon all the officers were occupied. You had blues, people demanding to be let out. It was just a shit fight.

'A lot of the cameras were blocked during the mayhem. People started standing in front of cameras. A woman was standing in line with the camera that was on Savvas. It was pretty clear she knew where it was and that she was attempting to obstruct the camera's view.'

Despite the woman's effort (hint, hint: she was a *leggy blonde*), the camera revealed part of the extraordinary escape.

'If you look real close you can see movement,' Chisholm continued. 'Savvas is taking off his overalls. He gets them off and dumps them on the floor. Then he whacks on a T-shirt and shorts. The footage also shows him putting on some sort of disguise . . . a moustache or whatever.'

In fact, Savvas not only slapped on a moustache – some claim made from hair he had cut from his head and glued to GLAD Wrap – he also expertly fitted a wig.

Remember his toilet trip?

Savvas is alleged to have secreted a Stanley utility knife, a razor and a shard of mirror inside his suit. While the woman and the two men shielded him from the camera, the drug kingpin used the blade to slice the cable tie holding his jumpsuit together and the mirror shard to look at himself while he affixed the moustache and wig. He also slid on a pair of sunnies.

Savvas then calmly stood and followed his two visitors out the door. *Easy.*

'He just cut himself out of his overalls and walked out of visits,' said Norris. 'I don't think there were the security checks that there should have been; it was all makeshift because of the renovations. They would have had a guy on the door to the crims area and another on the door at visits. There is no way he could have walked out of there wearing overalls, and he shouldn't have been able to walk through there at all.'

Chisholm said another woman staged a key distraction. 'Some officers were tied up with the blues, and others had to let the visitors out. Those officers handed the visitors over to another officer, who took them and passed them through a gate to another officer. They were then taken through a secure tunnel to a final checkpoint before going out.

'It was there that another stink kicked off. A woman claimed someone had stolen her purse from the locker they put valuables in before they are allowed into the jail. She was screaming about having $1500 stolen. She was going off her tree, which left the officer tied up while a whole lot of the other visitors were trying to push their way out.

'So [the officers] did their best and put them all out. Unfortunately, they put Savvas out too.'

So with a blond wig, a sliver of mirror, a razor and a mass distraction involving no less than eight people, George Savvas strolled out on his 30-year sentence in a maximum-security jail, jumped in a waiting car and disappeared . . .

The Conspiracy

Four days earlier . . .

Savvas walked straight up to the boss, cocky and confident as always. Bank robber, former escapee and all-around tough man Russell Cox was by his side.

'Good news, chief,' he said to Allan Chisholm, the boss doing his daily walk through the jail.

'Oh,' said Chisholm, 'and what would that be?'

Savvas smiled. 'You know that Royal Commission? Well, I've been called up to give evidence against the police. And it looks like the two fellas that arrested me might be in some shit, so I reckon I'll get a retrial. The worst they can do is find me guilty, but of a lesser degree. I might get 17 years, but with time served I'll be eligible for more visits, work, you know . . . the lot. I could even be out right away.'

And he *would* be out soon – but he never made it to his appointment with the Wood Royal Commission, a two-year investigation into police corruption that began in 1995.

'Savvas was some big player in the Labor Party,' Chisholm recalled. 'And he was involved in many things. He seemed to know all the big players in town, and if there was something dodgy going on, well, he knew about it. His sentence seemed a bit unusual and didn't sit well with me. He got a maximum of 30 years for conspiracy to import drugs. Thirty years, and he never actually imported them. That seems a bit heavy to me. [At the time he and Russell Cox approached me], he had already done 14 years.

'I wished him good luck and went on my way. That was on the Wednesday, and he was due to give evidence before the Royal Commission the following Tuesday. I was stunned when I found out he'd escaped on that Sunday – surely he would have preferred to leave as a free man?

'It was later revealed that Savvas, unoriginally and predictably described by the media as the "Mr Big of drug importation", had already been interviewed at length, and over a period of time, by the National Crime Authority. He had agreed to talk to them with the NCA offering the prospect of early release if he cooperated.'

The Mystery Blonde

The guards were stunned.

Who is this good sort? they thought as she signed her way into the visiting section. *And why the hell is she coming two hours from Sydney to see that putrid piece of scum?*

Wearing a short skirt, a tight top and a flirtatious smile, the intriguing visitor began appearing at Goulburn Jail in 2006, the exact date locked away in the Department of Corrective Services logbooks. The man she had been coming to visit was a notorious paedophile who was kept in protection for his own safety. The woman gave no clues as to why she would visit such a man, convicted of the most abhorrent crimes. Was she a relative? A friend? God forbid . . . *a lover?*

'We found out about this woman afterwards,' said Chisholm, who was in charge of the immediate investigation following the escape. 'I can't think of the paedophile's name, but he was a no good piece of shit. Anyway, this sheila would come down from Sydney to visit him. It just started out of the blue, and she kept on coming.'

Officers were further floored when they found out exactly how she was getting to Goulburn.

'Turns out she lived in Queensland,' said Chisholm. 'She used to fly to Sydney and then catch a taxi all the way to Goulburn. A taxi . . . You can only imagine how much that would cost.'

The leggy blonde had also rented a unit in Goulburn, and she was never short of company.

'Wives and girlfriends were always coming up to Goulburn to visit their men,' Chisholm said. 'Goulburn is a decent drive from anywhere, and this woman took advantage of that. She befriended a bunch of the visiting women and ended up getting a group of them together that she would put up in the unit for free. They would all stay in this unit on weekends so they could be close to the jail.'

Now for the schooners and sex . . .

'This woman,' Chisholm said. 'She was a good-looking woman. And it turns out she had gone to my deputy on the weekend before the escape and filed a complaint against one of my officers. She claimed the senior officer in charge of visits had harassed her. He had bumped into this woman down at the Soldiers Club and ended up screwing her. He was married but started having an affair with her.

'We figured that she would have been in a position to find out how everything worked in the visiting section from an officer's perspective. She would have known all the policies and all the procedures. She would have known the system inside-out, and she would have known how to create a distraction – a big distraction. If you look at the tape, she's the one obstructing the camera that was looking at Savvas.'

Chisholm concluded that the mystery woman had orchestrated the brazen escape – she had spent months in Goulburn planning and plotting before finally unleashing the chaos that allowed a wig-wearing, moustachioed Savvas to simply walk from the jail.

'I don't even think Savvas knew he was getting out,' Chisholm continued. 'Not until he met those two fellas that visited him anyway. We never got any intel on this, and we didn't know it was coming because this escape was not arranged by the inmates. It was very unique in that it was arranged by the *visitors*.

'The inmates had no idea what was happening. If any one of them had known about it then we would have known about it too. Jail is full of informants – someone would have given them up.

'The only people that knew about this escape was the woman that had organised it, the women that had been staying with her and were visiting on that day, and the two men that visited Savvas. Those two men were just nobodies. They used fake IDs to get in, and I don't think they'd visited him before. To my knowledge they were never found, nor were the women.'

So who would go to such lengths to bust Savvas free? If Savvas hadn't used a secret honey pot to pay for and organise his freedom, who had?

'There are all these stories about Savvas having all this money,' Chisholm said. 'But he didn't have any money. Not that sort of money, anyway. The government had seized his assets. It is a fallacy that he had all this money to pay all those people off. The police told me that. They were adamant it was not arranged by Savvas.'

That's when Chisholm gets all *Twilight Zone* . . .

Savvas's escape was front-page news . . . and someone needed to be blamed.

'The Minister of Corrective Services charged into my office,' Chisholm said. 'The cameras were all outside, media everywhere, and he stood in my office and told me everything would be fine if I gave him a head. He looked at me and said, "Give me someone." I refused.

'I had reviewed the incident and it was a failure of the system. There was no corruption or anything else on the part of the officers. The only bloke that played a role in it was the officer who rooted the sheila, and he had no idea what she was up to. But the minister wanted a head to give to all the reporters waiting outside. They wanted to show that the department had done something. I told him the only head I would give him was mine, and he took it. I thought I was invincible at the time; I was naive thinking I was too big to be blamed.'

Several investigations were launched – Corrective Services, the police, ICAC and the NSW Ombudsman – all examining the escape. The report released by NSW Ombudsman Irene Moss in December 1997 claimed Chisholm ignored intelligence given to him just weeks before the escape. Moss found the acting governor had made no obvious attempts to tighten security, despite tip-offs.

Corrective Services commissioner Leo Keliher revealed both Chisholm and his deputy Paul Lafoe were facing disciplinary charges over the escape shortly after the ombudsman's report was released. (The full report was never released publicly, just a four-page summary.)

'I got hammered,' Chisholm said. 'I was the first superintendent in history to have departmental action taken against him. There were charges but there was no punishment, which was convenient because that gave me no right of appeal. If I had been found guilty and was penalised in a way that disadvantaged me, then I would have had a right to appeal. Well, they found me guilty but took no further action – I wasn't suspended, docked, demoted and nothing was noted on my file.

'The ombudsman's inquiry found me guilty of negligence, but the police investigation found me innocent, and I was cleared by ICAC.'

Moss, however, was scathing in her report that no procedures were in place to ensure inmates were accounted for before visitors were allowed to leave: 'There was not even a thorough headcount of visitors arriving and those leaving.'

The report also pointed to intelligence that was ignored, saying, 'The department did have intelligence about possible escape bids by Savvas. He had been moved from Maitland Correctional Centre to Goulburn in January 1995 for precisely this reason. In June 1995, additional intelligence was gathered about the possibility of him escaping through the visitors section at Goulburn. While this information was, by the time of Savvas's actual escape, at least a year old, it was brought again to the attention of the governor as part of an updated profile of the inmate just weeks prior to the escape. In view of this, it is surprising that particular steps were not taken in relation to this inmate's visits, especially when visits were to be conducted in a temporary area. The governor noted that, in reality, all maximum-security inmates are a potential security risk and so if there is no particular intelligence available, or other suspicion, no additional steps are put in place.'

While the report could not rule out 'collusion', the ombudsman found administrative failings were to blame. A raft of high-tech changes were introduced in 'a bid to stop the top 100 high-risk prisoners in New South Wales from escaping. The measures introduced following Savvas's brazen escape included:

- No transport anywhere without the agreement of the newly formed High-Risk Management Committee (HRMC)
- Forced regular cell changes
- Visitors nominated in advance to enable thorough criminal record checks
- All nominated visitors to submit to a 'biometric visitor ID', a high-tech system involving photographs and fingerprints.

The sad footnote when the dust cleared and all the reports were filed was that Chisholm's career in Corrective Services was doomed. He claims he was shuffled through the system following the escape, his cards forever marked.

The Fox

The 'Black Fox' picked up the phone and dialed 000.

'Hello,' the man addressed the emergency operator. 'This is the Black Fox. George Savvas is dining at the Suntory restaurant on Kent Street if you want to go and pick him up.'

Click.

The line was dead.

'Attention all units,' the police two-way blared. 'Possible prison escapee spotted. Suspect may be armed and danger-ous. Approach with caution.'

Detectives Cameron Lindsay and Nick Read, cruising past Sydney Harbour Casino, agreed it was a long shot . . . but a shot all the same. The suspect allegedly spotted was, after all, Australia's most wanted man. They arrived at Suntory City – a fine-dining venue – at about 9pm.

'We attended the restaurant and spoke to the manager,' recalled Detective Lindsay. 'He was quite shocked, but he sat us down at a table behind the suspect.'

The detectives ordered a couple of Cokes and sat back, studying the man alleged to have been on the run for 258 days after escaping Australia's most secure jail. The man they watched was flanked by two good-looking women, eating beef fillets and sipping red wine. He had a beard and wore his hair short. They could not be certain of his identity, so Lindsay walked outside, made a call back to the Sydney Police Centre and asked for a picture of Savvas. A uniformed officer rushed the picture to the restaurant and Lindsay compared it to the suspect. And that's when they made their move and approached the trio's table.

'I am Detective Cameron Lindsay of the Rocks police. Could we please talk to you about certain matters outside, sir?'

Walking past the brimming bar, Detective Lindsay asked the bearded man with the short hair if he was George Savvas.

'No,' the man replied.

'Do you have any ID?' the detective continued.

'No.'

That's when Savvas bolted.

'Nick went in high and I went in low,' said Lindsay of the crash tackle that downed Savvas before the fugitive was handcuffed and pushed into the back of a paddy wagon.

'I suppose it was a bit stupid staying in Sydney,' Savvas blurted, his fling with freedom ending on a busy city street.

Police found $750 cash in Savvas's pocket, along with a gram of cocaine. There were also telephone numbers written on scraps of paper. The two good sorts back at the bar said they had known 'Andy' for a month or so. They were left with the $317.50 bill for the Wolf Blass and beef.

Just 59 days after his recapture, George Savvas was found dead in Maitland Jail. The drug-dealing former alderman was swinging from a sheet when prison officers unlocked his cell at 8.25am on 18 May 1997.

Savvas spent his last night alone, placed in isolation after authorities learned he was plotting another escape – this time with serial killer Ivan Milat. The attempt was to be far more elaborate, and potentially lethal.

'They were prepared to injure or kill anyone who got in their way,' said former prison official Ron Woodham. 'They planned to overwhelm guards in the top security unit, tie them up, steal their uniforms and then make their way to the perimeter wall. Rope ladders were going to be thrown over the wall by outside accomplices, with weapons and getaway cars.'

None of this happened, of course – authorities swooped after an alleged tip-off saw Savvas and Milat abandon the escape. Prison authorities, police and ICAC had been monitoring the plot for three weeks with hidden recording devices, informants and undercover agents.

'Operation Bengal', the name of the joint operation, left Savvas a broken man. Threatened with unprecedented surveillance and no prospect of freedom for possibly 30 years, Savvas turned his bedsheet into a noose, secured it to the metal bar of the inner security grille and hung himself.

Or did he?

Provocative questions have since been raised: Why wasn't Savvas found in his cell until 8.30am when wake-up time is 7 and breakfast is served at 7.45? Why was a man who was just threatened with unprecedented surveillance left unwatched and alone in a cell on the night his escape plan was foiled?

Why did no one even check on him since it is standard practice for an officer to make a cell check every 15 minutes when an inmate is in an observation cell?

Chisholm, now 'too old to care', has suspicions too: 'Stinks a bit to me. He tells me the Royal Commission is going to get him out, and then he escapes just before he is due to appear. Then he gets recaptured in a pub with a couple of prostitutes, cocaine and cash, the day after the Royal Commission finishes. And then all of a sudden he necks himself in Maitland Jail. Mmmm.'

9

RAPE and RAPISTS

Home and Away

The detectives walked into the prison hospital, notepads out but not optimistic they'd need them.

He won't talk. They never talk. Especially when it comes to this . . .

One of the officers pulled out a chair. 'Mind if I sit down?' he asked.

The inmate nodded and gently patted the bleached white blanket he was wrapped in. 'Go for it.'

Well . . . he didn't tell me to get fucked. That's a start.

The officer, now sitting as his copper colleague stood at the end of the bed, pulled a pen from his pocket and placed the notepad on his knee.

'So we hear you were admitted to hospital with some quite serious wounds,' the officer said. 'Would you like to tell us how you got them?'

The recovering inmate bashed him with a brow.

'You mean my arse?' he said, surprised by the beat-around-the-bush cop. 'Who ripped it open?'

Here we go then . . . Where's that pen?

The detective cut to the chase. 'Were you raped? Were you sexually assaulted by another inmate?'

'Of course I fucking was.' The prisoner laughed. 'Why else would I have needed 20 stiches in my arse. I was raped, raped and then raped some more. Go fuck up that piece of shit, that fucking rapist DOG.'

That notepad was needed after all.

'Well, some details first,' the detective said. 'We need to know exactly who did it, how they did and when they did it.'

The inmate nodded again. 'It happened at 7pm the first time – the first night of the lock-in.'

The officer's pen raced across the page.

'Oh, 7pm,' the officer said. 'And how can we confirm this? Were you wearing a watch? Maybe an alarm clock in the cell?'

The inmate looked stumped. 'No, I don't own a watch.'

The officer stopped writing. 'Well, how do you know it was 7pm?' he asked, the credibility of the victim suddenly a concern.

The inmate smiled. 'Easy. I was trying to block everything out when he threw me over the bed, but all I could hear was that bloody theme song from *Home and Away*. You know, "*Home and away . . . closer each day . . .*" I don't know what was worse, him pounding away or me having to listen to that shit. Anyway, it starts at 7pm, right?'

212

The detective nodded. And then he laughed.

To be fair to the detective, the inmate laughed first. The wounded prisoner was quite the comedian, as well as being a convicted rapist himself.

What goes around comes around?

'He was a scumbag,' said one Goulburn officer. 'He was a young bloke, sure, but he was in for brutally beating and raping a young girl. Anyway, he was sharing a two-out cell with another rapist, who just happened to be bigger, older and stronger.'

The rapist had taken advantage of a lockdown, according to the guard. 'They were shut in their cells for two days because of an incident. And this older rapist got stuck into the younger rapist for two days. It was quite brutal, and he didn't dob or complain – nothing like that. He just told an officer he needed to see the doc and was taken to the hospital when they found his anus had been torn apart.'

Now, this is graphic. Skip a paragraph if you must . . .

'He was at the hospital with his feet around his ears, getting his arse stitched up,' the guard continued. 'He said [the rape happened when] he was about to watch *Home and Away*. Apparently it was the attacker's favourite show and they watched it together every night.'

It can be revealed here that the man suspected with the *Home and Away* assault was none other than serial rapist Wayne Wilmot – one of the five men convicted of the notorious abduction, rape and murder of 29-year-old Cronulla bank teller Janine Balding in 1988. It was a crime that shocked the country.

Wilmot was released on parole after serving seven years for his role in the crime, only to be sent straight back to prison after attacking another woman at Leightonfield train station in Sydney's west in 1998. Wilmot has also been investigated for at least two other alleged sexual assaults while in New South Wales jails, in addition to being the suspected perpetrator in the *Home and Away* rape in Goulburn.

One of those alleged attacks was perpetrated against another convicted rapist, who was placed in a two-out cell with Wilmot in 2013.

'Wilmot was helping this guy with some basic maths,' the officer continued. 'He was teaching him how to do things like add and subtract. They had this bizarre little sex game that went with it, and every time the bloke would get a wrong answer, well, he would have to give Wilmot a quick suck or a lick. Anyway, the cellmate told officers that he'd got a few wrong answers in a row and Wilmot got carried away and ended up raping him in the mouth.

'Wilmot was moved down into the segregation unit after that. He is in a protection unit now, up behind the main jail. He has no remorse and is a complete predator.'

As we've learned, Goulburn Jail is the concrete fortress that stands between you and a chance meeting with Ivan Milat. The phone taps, the wire, the guards and the watchtowers protect you from serial killers like the Belanglo Butcher.

The green gate, the sandstone lion and the razor wire also stops jihadists from blowing you to bits, from machine-gun armed men maiming you in a massacre and from cult leaders cutting you to ribbons with clippers. And this prison – all legend and lethal – also keeps our worst sex offenders off the street.

They are as arguably more disgusting than any of the criminals you have met in the previous pages, and certainly more despised. One of them is a gang rapist named Skaf . . .

Porn

Heard the one about the gang rapist getting his hands on hardcore porn in prison? Yep. That's right. Bilal Skaf, the man who led a group of young men on a raping spree in Sydney's south-west and is serving 31 years for his crimes, had a pile of magazines under his bed.

He was batting over filth.

'I found a stack of hardcore porn in his cell three years ago,' said a current guard who asked not to be named. 'Most inmates are allowed to have soft porn in prison – pictures where all you see is pretty much boobs. But Skaf had a stack of horrible stuff in there. Now, that wouldn't be a big deal for most inmates, but when you are talking about a serial rapist that has never expressed the slightest bit of remorse for his crimes, it's a worry.'

Most people think Skaf is safely locked away in Supermax. He isn't.

'He was in the MPU when we found the porn,' the officer continued. 'He hasn't been in Supermax for a long time. He is not considered a high-risk inmate but is put in a protection wing for his own safety.

'He told me he didn't know where it came from and that it wasn't his, but there is every chance it came in through his privileged mail. We aren't allowed to check mail that comes from their lawyers or that is said to contain anything of a legal nature. This is a bit of a loophole that is taken advantage of, unfortunately.

'The privileged mail is scanned for metal objects like weapons, but anything else can get in, including phones, which aren't picked up by the metal detector. SIM cards don't get picked up, and neither do memory cards. It's not hard to slip those types of things into privileged legal letters.

'A lot of porn now comes into the jail via SD cards. But Skaf had magazines, the full-on X-rated type from overseas.'

Skaf has never been far from the spotlight, despite being locked away in Australia's most secure jail.

Skaf was initially sentenced to 55 years after being convicted on 21 counts of aggravated rape, assault and kidnapping. In 2000, he'd led 14 Lebanese–Australian Muslims on a series of gang rape attacks on Australian women. One of their victims was raped 25 times at Bankstown in an attack that lasted six hours. It's alleged she was called an 'Aussie pig' and told she'd be raped 'Lebanese style'.

'What this trial showed was that he was the leader of the pack, a liar, a bully, a coward, callous and mean,' said Judge Michael Finnane of Bilal Skaf in his sentencing remarks. 'The worst of all offenders who conducted himself as if the proceeding were a joke.'

Skaf began his sentence, which was later reduced to a maximum of 28 years on appeal, in Long Bay. He was placed in protection in 2 Wing after receiving death threats from fellow inmates.

Skaf still did not back down, though, despite being bashed by a guard and receiving death threats. He claimed that he started a gang while in jail called W2K – Willing To Kill – and threatened to shoot court officers and prison guards. He sent white powder in an anthrax hoax to prison boss Ron Woodham.

There were occasional cracks in the façade – Skaf also sobbed in his cell and attempted to commit suicide. His Long Bay horror ended – and a new one began – when he was transferred to Goulburn after prison authorities said three prisoners were plotting to inject him with a needle containing blood drawn from an HIV/AIDS-infected prisoner.

Skaf was embroiled in a fresh controversy shortly after arriving in Goulburn . . .

The prison officer walked into Cell 1, Unit 7, Supermax and saw scraps of paper lying on the bed. Bilal Skaf had been keeping busy . . . drawing. A new hobby perhaps?

The guard picked up the scraps, scanning his eyes over the drawings neatly executed in pen. He was horrified. The five cartoon-style pictures depicted all types of atrocities, among them his ex-girlfriend being gang-raped.

'Hurry up,' one of the cartoon rapists is saying to another. 'We have another 50 waiting.'

The explicit drawing also showed his former partner, who had stood by Skaf during his trial and conviction, being executed by a military-type character who is calling her a 'slut'.

The prison artwork horrified then prison boss Ron Woodham.

'Everyone who has seen them is shocked,' he said. 'During my career I have seen pornographic material crafted by inmates, but this is the first time I have seen drawings by a gang rapist encouraging gang rape. I believe the drawings depict the way he thinks. It tells you the way he thinks about women.

'He has learned nothing since his trial and conviction. He should take stock of the damage he has done to his victims and to their relatives. I've seen a lot of rapists show remorse and elect to do something about their offending behaviour. They have those options and they do exercise them. But he hasn't. He hasn't shown any remorse at all.'

The cartoons were placed in his prison intelligence file, as was the pornography found more recently in his segregation cell.

'Quick, get him out of there,' the officer ordered. 'They are going to rip him to bits.'

Skaf had begged and pleaded to be put in a wing with his 'brothers'.

'They love me,' he would tell officers. 'I'm their hero. I'm famous. They love what I did to those Aussie scum.'

At first his pleas fell on deaf ears. Skaf was not loved. He was hated. Most inmates wanted to kill the rapist grub on sight, and the officers did not want a death on their hands, even if it was Skaf's.

'About two years ago we put him in the Lebanese Yard,' said an officer who asked to remain anonymous. 'He really just stuck to himself; he hadn't been causing problems. He wanted to go back with his lot, and he was willing to sign a document saying he had no problems with anyone and he would be safe. The Lebs also said they wanted him in there, so management in all their wisdom got him out of segregation and put him in.'

A tip-off saved Skaf's life.

'He still thinks he is up there,' the officer continued, 'but he is considered a grub, even in the eyes of modern-day inmates. Anyway, he survived a couple of months, and then we got some information that he was about to get knocked. We quickly ripped him out of there and put him back into protection. Really, it was just luck that he didn't get killed – luck and some intelligence that was acted upon quickly.'

Bilal Skaf walks over to the wire fence and looks into the neighbouring yard.

'Hey, cunt!' he yells. 'Yeah you. You know I'm going to kill you.'

He spits, strongly but pointlessly given that his target is in the distance.

'Fuck you, Skaf!' the other inmate yells back. 'Fuck you. You are nothing but a rapist scum. Wait until I get my hands on you.'

This is the daily showdown that astounds the Goulburn guards. The mutual burning hatred has them baffled.

Why?

Because the man Skaf has made his number one enemy is none other than Robert Black Farmer, a sadist with a penchant for torturing women. Farmer is surely Skaf's equal when it comes to heinous crimes, having racked up 26 convictions by the time he was 25. Farmer was sentenced to a minimum of 20 years for brutally bashing Lauren Huxley with a fibro cutter before dousing her with petrol. He left Huxley to burn in her Northmead house. It was a crime that outraged a nation and, bizarrely, Skaf too.

'Skaf is a nobody,' another guard said, 'and he would be anonymous if it was not for his crime. The only thing that sticks out about him is his thing with Robert Farmer. Farmer is a scumbag, just like him, but for some reason they actually have a hatred of each other.

'We don't know where it comes from – maybe they don't either – but they want to kill each other. They are in separate yards in the same wing, both in protection, and they are equally hated. They scream at each other and issue threats through the fence.

'Farmer is one of the biggest girls you will ever meet. Every time we have dealings with him he cries. He will always mouth off first, but then he will cry like a baby when we put it back on him. He also pissed himself on one occasion, which you would expect from a weakling that goes around bashing and setting alight beautiful young girls.

'I haven't seen Skaf piss himself, but I am sure he has. He's very quiet and has limited dealings with others. It's a bit sad, really – the only person that has anything to do with him is his mum. She comes to visit, but that's it.'

While on the subject of piss . . .

'He likes to throw piss through the fence at Farmer,' said another officer familiar with Skaf. 'That is one of his favourite tricks. He pisses in his little milk container, takes it into the yard and then hurls it at him.'

For a bloke who thought he was popular, Skaf was also prepared for the worst. A Goulburn officer has revealed that the rapist is often armed.

'We found a decent weapon on him early in his stay,' the officer said. 'He had been on segregation, and when management thought he was ready he was moved. He was put into Unit 2. It was still a protection yard, but it was the first time he was going to be in a yard with anyone else. They were all what we call SMAPs (Special Management Area Placement crims), but Skaf must have been a little worried.

'The first day he came out into the yard, we did a search on him and found a crowbar in his towel. It was in his yard bag. He was asked why he had it, and he said, "Why do you think? It's my first day in the yard, chief. I have to arm meself up."

'He only had it to protect himself. He wasn't going to get anyone. He got moved down to the MPU after that and put back in segregation. After that they knew he couldn't be put in the yard, and he stayed in the MPU on protection until the Lebanese inmates put in a request for him to move into their yard.'

We know how that one went.

'And I Just Snapped'

The Goulburn officer cracked the lock. Then he pushed open the door.

'Out you get,' he said. 'Playtime in the yard.'

The prisoner moved his mouth, but nothing else. 'Might just stay here, chief,' he said, hands behind head and lying on his back. 'I couldn't be fucked.'

The officer stepped into the cell.

'You feel sick?' he said. 'You want the doc?' The officer was genuinely concerned. 'You okay?'

He took another step, the morning sun streaming into the cell, slapping him in the face. He squinted and looked behind him. A sticker on the back of the door grabbed his attention.

'And that is when I grabbed him by the throat,' the officer said. 'I ripped him from the bed and smashed him against the wall. I just lost it. I held him there – head rubbing concrete – and I choked him. I strangled him and wanted him dead.'

The message on the sticker? 'Life is Short.'

Nothing, right? Like a teenager slapping a Slayer poster on his wall or Ben Cousins getting some silly ink.

Wrong . . .

'Life is short?' the guard screamed into the inmate's ear, spit flying against face. *'LIFE IS SHORT?* Yeah, it's for the nine-year-old girl you killed. The one you fucking tied up and threw into a dam.'

The inmate could not respond. He was choking.

Ahhgg. Ahgg. Ahg.

The guard dropped his hand. The inmate continued to couch and cry as he cowered on the concrete floor.

'Not so tough when you're up against a man,' the officer shouted.'

The officer recalled the exact moment he wanted to kill Andrew Peter Garforth, the sexual deviant who had raped and murdered Ebony Simpson. Garforth even joined the police search for the girl, her ravaged body eventually found.

'I wanted to end him,' the officer said. 'That sticker just set me off. I absolutely lost my shit. I grabbed the bloke by the throat, I threw him up against the wall, and I choked him.'

Life is Short?

'Garforth was the fucker that murdered Ebony Simpson. She was only nine. He grabbed her on the way home from school, shoved her in his boot and drowned her in a dam. He tied her up with barbed wire before throwing her in. He fucking raped her too, and then he threw weights in her school bag and sent her to the bottom.'

The guard had held Garforth against the wall, the inmate frothing at the mouth as he gagged and gulped. He could have killed him. He *wanted* to kill him. But he suddenly stopped.

'To be honest, I don't know why I stopped,' the officer said. 'The only reason I reckon I did was because he started blubbering, and that made me feel good. He cried and begged. Maybe it was sadistic, but I enjoyed watching him cry and just told him he was a piece of shit and always would be. It was the satisfaction of seeing him crying that made me stop.'

Garforth is regarded as one of the most sickening men in Goulburn Jail. Several officers have been banned from working in his wing because authorities fear they may injure the convicted child killer.

'He is a putrid individual,' said another officer. 'He is a complaint merchant and whines all the time. He is in the boss's office complaining ten minutes after his cell is searched. He complains about everything. He says the officers messed up his cell and that he is being targeted unfairly. He is scared shitless of officers, though. He won't look at you in the face and certainly won't complain about anything that could lead to him being hurt.'

'He might be an even bigger target when the animals learn he is to blame for table tennis being banned,' the same officer continued. 'Not that it was really his fault.'

Garforth received a belting by table tennis bats soon after he arrived in Goulburn in 2001.

'He was bashed very badly,' the officer said. 'He was in the activities centre, and he got beaten up by a bunch of blokes that had armed themselves with table tennis bats.'

But couldn't you do more damage with your fist? Come on, a tiny table tennis bat?

'You have to understand these inmates are really different,' the officer continued.

'They aren't fisticuffs-type of people. They are all sex offenders and are all very cowardly. They won't punch with their hands. They are not big on violence but will use a weapon if they can get it to detach themselves from the violence of the act. They will use a weapon – anything they can get hold of – to make the violence seem okay.'

Oh . . . and they love a cheap shot.

'They are the type of people that will hit you from behind,' the officer said.

'They are cowards. They look at the ground most of the time, and Garforth is at the top of the tree when it comes to being a scared grub.'

Guarding paedophiles and child killers is without question the toughest job for any prison officer.

'You try not to look into their case history so you can remain professional,' said the officer who choked Garforth. 'They are hard enough to deal with when you don't even know what they've done. They are sickening in how polite they are. They try to be nice to the point that you want to throw up. There isn't a guard that doesn't have a story like my story. You are bound to snap around one of these predators. You don't want to, of course, and you restrain yourself as best as you can, but sometimes you just snap. It happens to everyone.'

This officer 'snapped', not only because of the sticker, but also because of a television special on Garforth's crime.

'Every now and then something will come up on TV, or in a newspaper, or even in conversation, and it will remind you of who they are and what they have done,' the officer said. 'It was about a week before I lashed out at [Garforth] that I saw a thing on him on a current affairs program. It was about the murder. Seeing that sticker and knowing he had murdered a beautiful little girl . . . How dare this putrid cunt have a sticker about life being short when he denied a little girl her entire life. It is not professional and I regret what I did, but sometimes you just snap.'

The child killer did not complain; sexual predators like this rarely do.

'He didn't make a complaint over what I did,' the officer said. 'They are just grubs, but you don't want to lose your job over them.'

A Fistful of Filth

Inmates are reluctant to lodge complaints against officers. They are even more reticent when it comes to pressing charges against fellow inmates.

'We had a couple of lock-in days back in 2009,' said a Goulburn officer. 'That's when the inmates are locked in their cells because of an incident or staffing issue. We found an inmate in a cell with horrendous injuries to his backside and took him to the hospital.'

The inmate confessed to being attacked, at least to the guards.

'He was in a two-out cell with a very infamous sexual offender. The guy told us that he had been tied to the sink and continually raped for the two days.'

But this was no normal rape.

'The poor bloke had been fisted,' the officer said. 'And that is both rare and disgusting, even for prison. He had been damaged in a big way and required lots of stitches. He had lost a lot of blood in the attack and could have been killed.'

But the inmate refused to cooperate with police. He said he would deny the attack if detectives were called.

'A lot of the time they won't press charges,' the prison officer continued. 'It depends on the crook – who he is and how long he is in there for. If they are doing a long time in jail, well, they won't press charges against another crim because they will get a reputation as a Dog. Their criminal career will be over if they are known as a Dog, and they will spend their time in jail in isolation. As crazy as it sounds, that is how it is.'

Officers often learn of sickening sexual attacks in jail but are powerless to seek justice on the behalf of the victim.

'We know a lot because of the injuries they suffer during the attacks,' the officer said. 'They are injuries that can't be hidden, and more often than not they would tell us how they got them.'

'However, we can't press charges on behalf of an inmate,' the officer continued. 'If an inmate comes to us with a busted arse, we can't do shit about it unless they tell us they are willing to pursue the matter with police. We can pass information on, but unless they are willing to cooperate, we have nothing and can do nothing.

'If they are ready to make the admission to the police, then it is escalated and their cell becomes a crime scene. DNA and evidence are taken from the cell.'

Who cares? They probably deserve it, right?

'Well, that's one way to look at it,' the officer said, 'but it really is an issue because the people that attack them never have a charge against them, and they can end up getting out of prison with everyone thinking they're reformed and that they're not going to be involved in another sex attack. That is clearly not the case if he has been raping men in prison.

'And a lot of these guys that are attacked end up committing suicide. That is something none of us want to see.'

Rapists v. Murderers

The convicted rapist pointed to the bulge near his belly.

'See that?' he boasted. '*See that?* Yeah. You know what that is?'

The other inmates – all child killers, paedophiles and prison scum – shrugged.

The rapist's brother, also convicted of a front-page sexual assault, butted in.

'It's a shiv,' he said. 'It's a big fucking knife. And we will stab you cunts unless you hand over your food. Unless you give us whatever you bought. Did any of you blokes get smokes?'

Then came a grunt.

'*MmmmaAAH,*' said one of the men in the middle of the jail yard shakedown. 'We will have to have a think about that.'

And think they did . . . for about an hour.

'So you want our buy-ups,' said the inmate who had approached the rapist turned shiv-wielding standover man. 'Well, we have thought about that and –'

Whack!

The rapist fell to the ground after being blindsided in the head by a plastic kettle.

His brother reached towards his pants . . . towards the shiv.

He was picked up from behind and pile-driven into the concrete.

Crash!

'*Arghhh*,' the brother screamed, grabbing his arm. It was badly broken, the bone having burst through skin.

ATTENTION. Fight in 2 Yard. I repeat . . . Fight in 2 Yard. Could all available guards respond.

'Two Yard?' An officer, who was part of a highly trained emergency response team, giggled. 'A fight in 2 Yard? What, has someone been hit with a handbag? Please. Haven't we got better things to do?'

'The radio call came over and everyone thought it was a gee-up,' one officer said, recalling the incident. 'Not because there aren't serious fights in jail – of course there are – but there are not serious fights in 2 Yard. This is where all the paedophiles and rapists are kept. They are protection inmates, and they are a bunch of weak-as-piss cowards. They don't fight. They *can't* fight.'

But the officers reluctantly responded to the call and rushed in.

And they were confronted by shocking scenes.

Oh shit! We are going to need gas! Quick, someone fire!

'It was on,' recalled an officer. 'We went in thinking an inmate was being cat slapped, and when we got there it was a full-on brutal bashing.'

'We looked across the yard and there were inmates just going crazy,' said another officer who witnessed the incident. 'They were jumping off tables and onto heads. They were hitting them with jugs. They were stomping and kicking. One of the brothers in particular was copping it.'

An officer screamed, 'Send in the gas. Fire!' But he was stopped.

'They couldn't use gas to stop it,' a guard revealed, 'because an officer had run through the back yard and grabbed one of the brothers, the one with the broken arm, and pulled him out. They couldn't fire while there was an officer in the yard.'

So the other officers went in, all ready for hand-to-hand.

'It was under control very quickly,' said an officer. 'From the time the radio call was given, it was stopped in about 30 seconds. They dropped to the ground like the cowards they are as soon as the squads poured in.'

The infamous Pakistani brothers, who had been sentenced to 32 years for a string of gang rapes committed on girls as young as 13 across Sydney in 2002, were in a seriously bad way. The brother who had been hit with the jug – a prisoner who can only be called MAK because of a court order – was still unconscious with head trauma. The other brother – a fellow known as MSK and the ringleader of the gang rapists – was sobbing in a corner, his arm busted to bits. The officers, seeing the seriousness of MAK's condition, immediately ran over to him.

'Oh, he was fucked,' said one of the responding officers. 'There was blood everywhere. And this bloke had brains coming out of his ear. Seriously, there was grey matter on the ground. They had stomped the shit out of him. The officers got in quick, but it had been going on for about a minute or so before they arrived. And that is a lifetime when it comes to a jail attack. We worked on him for a good ten minutes before the ambulances came, but his brains were all over the floor. It was brutal, just putrid.'

The incident became headline news – 'Rapists v. Killers', one leading newspaper screamed.

'Two notorious Pakistani gang rapist brothers are in a critical condition in hospital after being bashed in a brawl involving seven of the state's worst offenders at a high-security jail,' reported Sydney's *Daily Telegraph*. 'It is understood MAK started the melee when he stabbed another inmate with a pen. MAK suffered severe head injuries and was transferred from Goulburn to Canberrra Hospital, where he was operated on just hours after the fight erupted at 12.30pm on Thursday.'

Seven men were charged with the 8 February 2007 bashing – among them were Matthew Wayne de Gruchy, who killed his mother and two siblings in 1996; Craig

Andrew Merritt, serving 27 years for suffocating his three children; Jay William Short, who killed a teenager in Lithgow before burying her in a sandpit; and Shannon Daley. They were all convicted of charges including maliciously inflicting grievous bodily harm, assault occasioning actual bodily harm, and common assault.

'The guys that attacked them weren't a gang. They just banded together to fight a common cause. They didn't belt these blokes because they were rapists, as some believe . . . They fought them because they were trying to stand over other inmates. It was yard politics. They claimed to have a shiv. We watched the CCTV afterwards and you can clearly see that they were motioning towards the front of their pants. And if you have a shiv in the yard, you are either a boss or you are bashed. These blokes bashed them because they didn't want the brothers to have any power over them in the yard.'

The attack was described as the most brutal protection bashing in Goulburn's history.

'It was one of the worst violent attacks I have seen,' said another officer. 'The MAK guy, he is still bad. He was left with brain damage and he can't even construct a sentence now.'

Select Bibliography

Bayley, R., 'The Settlement of old Goulburn', *Goulburn Post*, 27 February 2013

Bearup, G., 'George Savvas's $317 meal to remember', *Sydney Morning Herald*, 22 March 1997

Bissett, K., 'Savvas tip-offs failed to stop escape', *Daily Telegraph*, 17 December 1997

Corrective Services NSW, *Offender Classification and Case Management Policy and Procedures Manual, 12.3 Category AA and Category 5 Inmates*, December 2013

Dalton, V., 'Prison homicide in Australia: 1980 to 1998', Australian Institute of Criminology, February 1999

Davies, L., 'Life alone for killer in Supermax', *Daily Telegraph*, 23 August, 2010

Davies, L., 'Sydney sharia whipping case: man jailed for dishing out 40 lashes', *Sydney Morning Herald*, 14 June 2013

Doherty, L., 'High security prison to house the very worst', *Sydney Morning Herald*, 2 June 2001

Fife-Yeomans, J., 'Radicals run riot', *Daily Telegraph*, 22 September 2014

Fife-Yeomans, J., 'Charges laid over jail riot', *Daily Telegraph*, 17 October 2014

Gibbs, S., 'Hard men turn to Islam to cope with jail', *Sydney Morning Herald*, 19 November 2005

Gilmore, H., 'Inmates studying al-Qaeda manual', *Sun Herald*, 2 December 2007

Hills, B., 'How bikie ran gang from his jail cell', *Sunday Telegraph*, 17 November 2013

Kennedy, L., 'Warders hurt in prison riot', *Sydney Morning Herald*, 17 April 2002

Kennedy, L., 'Blonde wig and glasses – how Savvas fooled prison warders', *Daily Telegraph*, 8 July 1996

Kerr, J., 'Goulburn Correctional Centre: a plan for the conservation of the precinct and its buildings', commissioned by NSW Public Works for the Department of Corrective Services, September 1994

Lewis, D., 'High tech jail escape barriers', *Sydney Morning Herald*, 20 July 1996

Lipari, K., 'X-rays could net Milat $40,000', *Daily Telegraph*, 30 October 2002

McIlveen, L., 'Worst killers get a jail of their own', *The Australian*, 2 June 2001

Masters, C., 'Supermax', *Four Corners*, ABC, 7 November 2005

Mercer, N., 'Torture, and having to eat brown bread – the

extraordinary complaints about life in Supermax',
Sunday Telegraph, 7 October 2007

Mitchell, A., 'Milat, Savvas jail break-out foiled', *Sun
Herald*, 17 May 1997

Mitchell, A., 'Inside story of Savvas: the mystery of the final
hours', *Sun Herald*, 25 May 1997

Mitchell, A., 'Cartel links to jail killing', *Sun Herald*,
2 November 1997

Mitchell, A., 'Mastermind recruiting gang inside super jail',
Sun Herald, 22 April 2007

Morton, J., *Maximum Security: the Inside Story of Australia's
Toughest Gaols*, Pan Macmillan, Sydney, 2011

Moss, I., 'The Savvas report: a special report to Parliament
under section 31 of the Ombudsman Act/NSW
Ombudsman', December 1997

Moss, I., 'Report on investigation into the introduction of
contraband into the High Risk Management Unit at
Goulburn Correctional Centre', ICAC, February 2004

Silmalis, L., 'Milat sparks escape scare', *Sunday Telegraph*,
11 May 2003

Spaccavento, B., Dowel, N., Quilkey, C., 'Custody and
Sentence Planning – a through care model for "AA"
inmates', *Australian Journal of Correctional Staff
Development*

Sutton, C., 'The new $22m home for our most evil men',
Sun Herald, 27 May 2001

Tonkin, S., 'Girlfriend used condoms to smuggle
phones, cables into Goulburn Jail', *Illawarra Mercury*,
23 September 2014

Vass, N., 'Jailers seize drugs', *Sunday Telegraph*, 21 April 2002

Wallace, M., 'A fake gun but no empty threat', *Daily Telegraph*, 7 August 2004

Watson, R., 'Guns, drugs, rope, lip gloss must-have items behind bars', *Daily Telegraph*, 16 May 2009

Watson, R., 'Killers, madmen, me and Ivan Milat – inside Supermax', *Daily Telegraph*, 9 May 2009

Watts, B., Lawrence, K., 'Smirking inmate drug ring charges', *Daily Telegraph*, 6 December 2008

Acknowledgements

At first I was met with silence. 'I'm not talking to you,' they said. 'And no comment.' But slowly and surely the brave men and women who have worked in Goulburn Jail came forward with their remarkable stories. I would like to thank each and every person who fronted up to break a culture of silence to contribute to this book. Many of you asked to remain anonymous, and that is how you will stay. Sorry to those of you whom I mobbed in the street or door-knocked, and more so, thanks for not swatting me with a broom or chasing me from Goulburn with a pitchfork. I can't name many of you, but I can name some. In no particular order I would like to thank Ian Norris, Al Chisholm, Dave Farrell, Grant Turner and Kevin Camberwell. All these men are former Corrections officers and bloody legends – thanks for your service and your friendship.

To Tim Swain, you are an inspiration, mate. What happened to you was just shit, but your recovery, your strength and the way you confront each day is simply brave. Thanks for trusting me with your story. The same goes to Jane Swain. I am sure Tim would have not let me in the door had it not been for you. Thanks for everything.

Also a special shout-out to John Heffernan. The 'Last Governor' has backed me and supported me from day one.

The great men who helped me with my last book, *Australia's Hardest Prison: Inside the Walls of Long Bay Jail*, also helped me with this one. Roy Foxwell put me in touch with Al Chisholm, who was a very big part of this book. Al had never spoken about his controversial stint as governor of Goulburn, and he may never have if it wasn't for Roy. Thanks 'Foxy' . . . again.

Thanks to 'Dave the Dentist'. You put me in touch with a bloody legend and also look after my teeth.

I also spoke to several men who have lived their lives on the other side of the law. Thanks for telling me your stories and trusting me to keep your identities safe.

I also have to thank *Daily Telegraph* sports editor Tim Morrissey and *Sunday Telegraph* sports editor Chris Hopper for allowing me to take time out from chasing cars and footballs to chase criminals. A special thanks goes to you, Tim, for supporting me even though I used to be a very messy desk-mate. I would like to thank Mick Carroll, who is the reason why I am still a journalist. So yes, Mick, you're to blame.

Thanks to my one and only publisher, Alison Urquhart. We have done it four times now! Thanks for backing me once again. And to Brandon VanOver; we have only met once but

ACKNOWLEDGEMENTS

you know me so well. Thanks for your kind, thoughtful and diligent editing. You made it painless.

And lastly, thanks to my family. As always, I do this for you.

Read on for an extract from *Australia's Hardest Prison: Inside the Walls of Long Bay Jail*

Not all escapes are successful, no matter how clever or original they are. Sometimes the most brilliant bids for freedom are foiled by complex investigations and crafty cunning. But most of the time, it's just dumb luck.

Let's take a look at Long Bay's Best of the Busted.

Banging Boots

'He'd come up with a pretty ingenious plan to escape.'
Long Bay guard

The guard at reception placed the jacket, the shirt and the tie on the counter.

The inmate looked at him. 'What about me shoes?' he asked.

'Yeah, right. I forgot about them,' said the guard. He picked up a pair of black boots from the locker and brought them to the prisoner. 'Here they are,' he said, slapping the soles of the boots together before putting them on the counter.

The inmate dived to the floor.

'What the hell are you doing?' said the guard, looking down at the prisoner, who was crouched with his hands over his head.

Eric Heuston, the inmate picking up his clothes for a morning court appearance, wiped the dumb look from his face and picked himself up from the ground.

'Jeez, chief,' he said. 'I thought you were going to throw them at me.'

But Heuston didn't think his boots were about to be thrown from the air. He thought they were going to explode . . .

Heuston went back to his cell. He dumped his clothes on the end of the bed and sat for a while, wondering if his plan would work.

So far so good, he thought.

He held a boot in each hand; his right was holding a bomb, his left a detonator.

'Eric had his clothes brought in by a friend before his court appearance,' said a former guard. 'Part of the normal jail process is that you pick up your civilian clothes the night before your court appearance. The crims would shower before they went to bed and get up early and change so that they'd be ready for their escort.'

But Heuston was not planning on getting on a bus in the morning. He was going to get out tonight.

'He'd come up with a pretty ingenious plan to escape,' the guard said. 'He'd got his friends to make some special boots for him. The big chunky heels were hollowed out, and gelignite was put in one and a detonator in the other.'

With his 'banging boots', Heuston was ready to go. He walked out of his cell, across the landing and down the stairs to ground floor. He walked right up to the end of the remand centre, to the wall made of glass brick. Heuston assumed it was the weakest point of the building and was now ready to blast his way out. Taking the boot that held the explosive, he placed it at the bottom of the wall. Grabbing the other, he made his way down the hall until he was close enough to detonate the bomb, but far enough not to explode himself. He took one more look at the wall to make sure nobody was in harm's way then –

Boom!

The shoe exploded. Glass, leather and wood flew into the air. The noise shattered the evening silence and the inmates roared. The smoke slowly cleared and Heuston was primed for his getaway. He was thinking about the snipers in the towers as he ran towards the smashed wall. Well, at least he thought it was smashed . . .

'The blast was big,' the guard said. 'It made a hell of a noise and a huge mess, but it wasn't powerful enough to blast through completely.'

So Heuston was left standing there, detonator in hand and nowhere to go. He ended up in court the next morning, presumably without shoes, and would have to go back again soon to face another charge – attempted escape.

About the Author

James Phelps is an award-winning senior reporter for the *Daily* and *Sunday Telegraph* in Sydney. He began as an overnight police rounds reporter before moving into sport, where he became one of Australia's best news-breaking rugby league reporters.

James became News Australia's Chief National Motorsports writer and travelled the world chasing F1 stories, as well as becoming Australia's No. 1 V8 Supercar reporter. James is also a senior feature writer for the *Sunday Telegraph*.

Following the bestselling *Dick Johnson: The Autobiography of a True-Blue Aussie Sporting Legend*, James returned to his roots to delve into the criminal underworld with *Australia's Hardest Prison: Inside the Walls of Long Bay Jail* and *Australia's Most Murderous Prison: Behind the Walls of Goulburn Jail*. James is a twice V8 Supercar media award-winner and a former News Awards 'Young Journalist of the Year' and 'Sport Reporter of the Year', as well as a Kennedy Awards finalist for 'Sports Reporter of the Year'.

Loved the book?

Join thousands of other readers online at